FRECKLES

RON WEBER

PAGE PUBLISHING, INC.
Conneaut Lake, PA

First originally published by Page Publishing 2021

ISBN 978-1-6624-2083-2 (pbk)
ISBN 978-1-6624-2084-9 (digital)

Printed in the United States of America

ACKNOWLEDGMENTS

Thanks to my mother, June Weber, who raised me. She also taught me to write so I could tell all my readers how hard Freckles was on her. Sorry, Mom. Additionally, I have a tremendous amount of gratitude for my wife, Lydia, and her patience with me. At seventy-two years old, I think I have finally grown up with her help.

CHAPTER 1

HA HA HA

As a skinny red-haired kid with globs of freckles, I always wanted to be Superman. Alas, everyone who saw me couldn't help calling me Freckles. Although it was a name I hated, I was stuck with it for eternity. During the day, I was Freckles. When I closed my eyes and went to sleep at night, I was Superman. In school, when I was bored listening to the Catholic nuns who tried vainly to teach this hyperactive little kid, I would find myself far up in the sky with my blue suit and red cape, catching bad guys and saving the world.

I do not remember coming out, but a friend of mine always claimed he remembered doing just that. He said he remembered the bright lights, the doctor's stern face, the spank, the first breath, and the first cry. As for me, I just knew I had to get out right now. In just under six months in the womb, I wanted out. There were things to do, places to go, and people to meet. The doctors said we would both die, mother and child. In 1948, a premature baby, born in six months, was not given much of a chance. Often the mother died too. Somehow, we both survived.

If I could remember, I would see the insides of a huge washing machine. When I grew up, they would tell me it was called an incubator. In those days, they were several feet in diameter, with a small windowed hole for the crying mother to look into. Outside would be a skinny woman with a pale white face, red Irish hair, and a wrinkled face, staring in. She wasn't crying—she was laughing and smoking a cigarette. Having a premature baby would get her a lot of sympathy and attention from the local Catholic Church and all its seemingly devoted members. The smoke from her cigarette would blur my vision. However, my vision was already somewhat obscured from something that decades later would be called fetal alcohol syndrome. It's no wonder I go to AA meetings today, all these years later. Mostly, she just stared into the machine when people walked by. She wasn't looking at anything. Rather, she was making sure that people saw her looking in. Later, I would find out that was what good Catholics did in those days. They were always looking around, making sure others saw them—saw them at church, saw them at school, saw them kissing their babies, and saw them laughing and smiling as though everything were just fine. She would laugh in her cute little Irish way, "Ha ha ha. Isn't my baby cute? I hope he lives. Ha ha ha." Really, I am not sure if she cared at all. In fact, if I died, all the Irish people in the family could get drunk and feel sorry for her. She would dress up real pretty, light up a cigarette, pour a drink, and walk out of the kitchen with a big smile on her face. Ha ha ha.

"Thank you all for coming. You shouldn't have. I'm sure you have more important things to do than come to my son's silly funeral." Ha ha ha. "Can I pour you a drink? Let me get you an ashtray." Ha ha ha.

When she laughed, she always gave this forced little smile. You never knew if she meant it or not. Her eyes would roll around, looking anywhere but at you. Her smile would show itself, and out came "Ha ha ha." It sounded like one of those battery-powered talking dolls. When you pull the little cord, it always sounds exactly the same.

While mom and I survived, I only weighed three pounds and two ounces at birth. A week later, I was a whopping two pounds and four ounces. What's wrong with this picture? The doctors decided my mother's milk was not cutting it. I am glad they took me off it. If I could remember back that far, I probably would remember the taste of Irish whiskey in my milk. From the way I was losing weight, maybe I should have started a new fad diet: Drink all the milk and whiskey you want and still lose weight. Then I would remember being put back in the big washing machine for good—no more trips out for a milk-and-whiskey run. It's too bad I couldn't walk yet. I could stand up and pretend to be looking out at the woman who was pretending to be looking in at me. Even if I could, I don't think I could do that head-and-eye trick she did. It is a matter of pointing your head toward something and then moving your eyes to the sides as far as possible to see who is watching you pretend to look at whatever you are supposed to be looking at or doing whatever you are supposed to be doing. Even if I could have done that, I didn't have an audience watching me. I was alone in the big washing machine. Later on, in my boyhood, I would learn how to do that trick. The only time you didn't do it was in the confessional line. You didn't want anyone seeing you in that line—eyes on the floor and no looking around. Get back in your seat in with the others and don't tell anyone what you said to Fr. Schaefer in the confessional. Bad Freckles.

Finally, I got out of the big washing machine. They took me to a large house and gave me to an old woman. They called her Nanny. Later, I would find out her name was Mrs. Dolan. She beat my brothers and sister with a wooden spoon. I was too little, they told me. I had to be a big boy to get hit. I couldn't wait. Finally, another face showed up. The other two were women. This one was different. His name was Dad. His breasts were too small, and his chest was hairy. I hoped he didn't try to breastfeed me too. I was tired of sucking on dry nipples. My mother kept trying to do it herself until Dad hit her in the breasts and told her to stop. He said it looked disgusting, and Nanny had to do it. When she couldn't, it was back to the old bottle. But at least the milk in the bottle didn't taste like Irish whiskey.

My earliest memories included breathing lessons. My oldest brother, Rick, used to hide me from my mom. He called it babysitting and wanted money for it. He would hide me in cabinets, cupboards, and anywhere else she couldn't find me. One time my mother saw him putting me in a cupboard, alongside the pots and pans. When she yelled and told Rick that I couldn't breathe in there, he would open the door every few seconds and say, "Okay, Ron, breathe" and promptly close the door again. Once, Rick and my other brother Bob decided to hide me on the roof. They opened an upstairs window to a roof over the front door and helped me climb out. Then they promptly locked the window behind me. Although it was cold out there in December, the view was terrific. A neighbor called and told my mom that her baby was on the roof. "Ha ha ha," my mother said and hung up the phone. I can still hear her screams and remember the terrified look on her face through the window a few minutes later. It was sort of like when she looked at me through the incubator window, only this time it was her on the inside and me on the outside looking in at *her* for a change. Too bad I didn't have a cigarette and glass of Irish whiskey. I could have pretended to be looking in at her and hoped someone saw me. I would have thought it was funny and laughed back, "Ha ha ha." Watching her try to climb through the window and grasp at me with those arthritic, skinny, little Irish hands was even funnier. Rick and Bob would stand behind her, making funny faces at me.

The first time I heard her tell them, "Wait until your father gets home," I watched their faces change. Their smiles turned upside down. They turned upside down. When I got older, I would learn that it was called a frown. They knew they were going to get the belt when Dad got home. A few years later I would get the belt too. Ouch! The only funny part about it was watching my drunken father try to get the belt back in all the loops on his pants. He always seemed to miss a few. Maybe that was so he could pull the belt off faster when he was mad.

On Sundays we went to church. Good Catholics always went to church on Sunday. Dad used to like church too. He could drink beer on the way to and from. During the sermon, he would "go to the bathroom." He and some other men went together. The priest would always frown when they got up. They were supposed to listen to his sermon. When Dad came back from the bathroom, he always smelled like cigarettes and whiskey. Then he would go to sleep. Sometimes I did too. His snoring would wake me up, and all the people would look at us. My mom had this other trick I liked. She could talk through her teeth. A lot of the women at the church could do the same thing. By doing that, they could look like they were smiling at their husbands, when they were actually balling them out.

"Come on, honey, wake up, you're embarrassing us," she would mutter with her teeth closed tight and a big Irish smile. Sometimes her white teeth were all red from the lipstick where she missed when putting it on early that morning. She was late and in a hurry. After all, it was hard dragging your husband from one bar or party to another on Saturday nights. The worst part was when he would wake her up in the middle of the night because he couldn't sleep—lucky for the all-night pharmacy. I wonder how Dr. Harpole could stand all those late-night calls for prescriptions. I remember riding to the all-night pharmacy with them one time. It was kind of fun. The car would weave all over, bouncing off the curbs and other things. It was like the bumper car rides at the park. My mother would grit her teeth and hold on to the dashboard. She could hiss like a snake.

"*Hiss.* Bob, you're on the sidewalk. *Hiss.* Bob, you hit another mailbox. *Hiss.* Bob, you're going into the ditch." Dad would use big words I never heard before.

He would say things like, "Dammit, June, I said phenobarbital. I wanted phenobarbital. Why did he give you this other crap? This stuff constipates me. I need something to put me to sleep."

Then Mom talked, "*Hiss.* The doctor knows it's for you. Why do I have to lie and pretend the drugs are for me? Why don't you call him yourself? You just ran a red light. *Hiss.*"

Then Dad would hit her, and it was quiet for a few minutes. Mom was really strong. She never cried when he did that. When we got home from the pharmacy, I smelled like cigarettes and felt sick. They used to like to put all four of us in the back of the car, roll up the windows, and smoke. There were no windows in the back of our cars to roll down. Sometimes there was so much smoke in there, we could hardly see one another. Mom smoked these horrible-smelling menthol cigarettes, and Dad liked Philip Morris, the ones without filters. He died of alcoholism and lung cancer. She died of emphysema. Go figure.

When I was five, I got to go to the Catholic school. My sister, Rosalind, was a year older than me. She would walk me to the bus. She apologized to her friends for me and said she had to keep an eye on me. I had already left the house alone once, and they did not want that to happen again. I was only about three or four. This was the first of my many attempts at running away. I went two doors away to a house where some new people moved in. The woman was young and pretty. She had beautiful long, red hair, a cigarette in her hand, and a drink. She had a big smile and laughed, "Ha ha ha." It sounded real. She was young too. Hello, Mom. This was also my first attempt at finding my real parents. I knew they were out there somewhere.

"Aren't you a cute little boy? What's your name?"

"Leslie."

"Hi, Leslie, my name is Pat. You sure have pretty red hair and freckles. Why don't you come in for a cookie and lemonade?" Cookies and lemonade? I was movin' in.

I spent the next fifty years visiting Pat. She always had time to sit and chat—cigarette, drink, and all. It didn't matter what time—day or night—she always had a great smile, a hug, and a genuine laugh. Most important of all, she had time. She always wanted you to come in and chat with her. When I was grown up, someone told me she was lonely. Her husband hid in the basement, drinking all the time. It seemed like all the men I would ever meet in my life went to the basement to drink and hide. Were they bad? Did their wives send them down there?

Finally, a woman came banging on the door. She was breathing hard and did not have a drink or cigarette in her hand. I wondered why.

"Have you seen a little boy? He has red hair and freckles and is about three-and-a-half years old. His name is Ronnie." *Nice of you to drop by, Mom. I've been down here for two hours.*

"No, I haven't. I'm sorry. There is a little boy here named Leslie, but no Ronnie. I'm sorry. I hope you find your little boy. I hope he's not lost in those big woods out back."

"Leslie? Can I see what he looks like?" *Oops. Busted. Maybe I should have tried* George.

"Ronnie, what are you doing? You scared me to death. I looked everywhere for you. Why did you run away? Why did you tell this nice lady your name was Leslie?"

Good thing I was a slow talker. I just played dumb and smiled. *I mean, figure it out, lady. I go to where someone talks to me and plays with me for the first time in my life, and you want to know why?*

We had to get up very quietly each morning. Mom and Dad had another one of those big words. It was called a *hangover*. I wasn't sure why they called it that. In high school, Rick told me it was because they fell down a lot and had to hang on to things, like railings and toilet bowls. Nanny told me that my father was entertaining people at the bars all night. He sold insurance and had to get people drunk so they would buy his insurance. Mom had to go with him. It was easier to lie if you had your wife with you. Being Catholic, they could say whatever they wanted and then confess it all on Sunday. He would tell them all about why they should buy his insurance and no one else's. His was a better deal, and you got more for your money, he said. Mom smiled and agreed. Ha ha ha. He would get them drunk and have them sign papers. The next morning, everyone forgot all about it. Then my dad would wait for some big words like *premiums* and *renewals*.

On the way to school one day, Rick taught me another big word. It was called *accident*. He told me I was one. I told my teacher. All the kids laughed, and she called my mom. When Rick heard, "Wait until your father gets home," he started to cry. I guess I wasn't supposed to know that I was an accident. When I was older, and my father was gone, I asked Mom again. She told me that Dad didn't want any kids. When I asked her why he had four, she explained another one of her tricks. Catholics are really smart. When Dad was in WWII from 1940 to 1945, he was on a Merchant Marine supply ship for a year and then come back for a few weeks before going again. Each time he came home, he had a baby. He and Mom would drink and go to the bedroom a lot, and then he would go back to his ship. When he came home a year later, he had another kid. So after this happened twice, and the war was finished, he thought having kids was easy. He wanted a girl now, and then that was it. They went back to the bedroom a lot, and about a year later, they had a beautiful little girl. That's my sister, Rosalind. That was it—no more kids. He didn't want any, and now he had three—two boys and a girl. Poor Dad. Happy Mom.

"So what about me, Mom? I am the youngest. I'm the fourth. How did I get here?"

"Don't ask."

"Was Rick right? Was I an accident?"

"You were a surprise."

"Was I bad? Is that why I had to go in the big washing machine?"

"Stop asking about it, or I will tell your father."

"He doesn't live here anymore."

"Oh, that's right."

CHAPTER 2

CATHOLICS

I was born into a family that had a long and rich Catholic background. I say *rich* because the church tried to take all our money. They also got all the money from anyone else they could. As a child, I often heard that the more you dropped in the bucket, the more you could sin and get away with it. If you didn't sin a lot, you would get to sit closer to God and Jesus in the big church in the sky. They couldn't find a priest to bless me in the hospital. He was out getting drunk, committing sins, and stuff like that. My parents couldn't take me home until I was blessed. I waited three months in that hospital incubator before I was well enough to go home. Finally, the priest ran out of money and had to come back to the hospital. My dad gave him a twenty. He mumbled some gin-fouled words over me, and I got to go home. The priest got to leave too. Someone said he went to Florida to dry out in some private rehab place. When I finally did get home, the house I would grow up in had more statues, religious pictures, Bibles, and other related religious paraphernalia than the Vatican. Later I would find out it was because my parents were really bad. They needed all the help they could get.

The hardest part was when you came out of the confessional. You had to manage to walk all the way back to your seat in the church pew with your eyes looking at the floor. If you looked up, you might see that someone saw you. Then they might smile and say, "My god, you were in there a long time. What did you do?" But then everything was fine. On your way up to the communion railing, once again, you could smile, look around, and nod at all the people who saw you being a good Catholic and taking your communion. It was the same on the way back to your seat. You were done now. Your sins were all forgiven for that week. You had finished your penance of three "Our Father's" and two "Hail Mary's," and three "Glory Be to the Father's," and you had swallowed your communion host—no chewing now. Biting God is rude. Just swallow him, sip the wine, and go back to your seat. Grabbing the chalice from the priest and taking large gulps were frowned on. If you were an adult, there was plenty of time and booze in the car to do that on the way home. On the way back from communion, be sure to smile and nod at all the people as you go by. When you sit back in your seat, your job is to look at all the people going by, looking to see that you are looking at them. Nod, smile, and let them know you saw them being good. You were all forgiven and saved for that week. As soon as you got home, you could start sinning all over again. God bless the Catholic Church. I am lucky I was born into it, because everyone else was going to hell. At least that is what I was taught for eight years of grammar school, four years of high school, and one semester of college. After flunking out of a Catholic college, I was the scourge of the family. I had to join the army and hide for three years. I wonder if God will ever forgive me. Am I really going to hell? At least some of the neighborhood kids will be there with me.

Another humorous part of the church service was the money collection. Right after the sermon, several men would pass these long-handled baskets throughout the large church. While I have seen other congregations just pass baskets that are handed around by the congregation and then collected at the back of the church, that was not the case here. Doing it this way would make it easier for the slackers to just pass the basket without putting anything in it. In my church, these stern-looking men in suits would put the basket in front of you and then not move it until you put something in it. Then one by one, each person faced the grim reaper. Pay up or else. The funny part of the whole affair was *who* would get to pass the buckets. While only about ten men were needed, there was always a scuffle about who they would be. The basket passers were allowed to go to the rear of the church just before the priest would begin his long and boring sermon. At the rear of the church, they would decide who took which basket to which part of the church. As this took some discussion, they were allowed to walk outside the front doors of the church and talk quietly. Conveniently, while this was taking place, the cigarettes and booze came out. Once their decision was reached, they would wait until the sermon was over and then walk to their designated spots. Not only did they miss the sermon, but they also got a smoke and a drink. However, when they got outside the front doors, there was about thirty men standing there. The conversation went something like this:

"I'll do it."

"No, I'll do it."

"No, no, that's okay, guys, Fred and I will get it today."

"No, really, I don't mind, Steve and I can get it."

"But you guys did it the last three times. Let someone else do it."

"Let's go have a smoke and talk about it."

"Great. Hey, I've got a bottle under the seat."

"Okay, let's go."

After the sermon, a large group of men would stagger back in, smelling of gin, Irish whiskey, and cigarettes. The winners would grab the baskets, and the rest would go sit down next to their angry wives. The priest would stop his boring sermon that he had read twice already that day at earlier services, long enough to frown at the men. I think he was just jealous because he hadn't had a drink since just before the service started and had to wait until communion to get another one. I used to love the way those guys would dispense the wine after giving out the hosts. They would tip it up just a bit and then yank it back before you could get very much. You see, in a Catholic church, the wine that was blessed had to be completely dispensed. Because of some holy ritual, they couldn't have any leftover. So whatever we didn't get, he did. If he held back enough, he could get a couple of real big swallows. As an altar boy, I could see his eyes get big when he realized there was still about a pint of wine left in that huge chalice. I would hear several large swallows, followed by a big burp and then a big sigh of relief as all that booze hit the old stomach. They always made it like they were wiping their mouth off with that blessed little, white towel. Actually, they were covering their mouth while they did the big belch.

When I was about twelve years old, I was an older altar boy. The priests stared at me differently now. I complained about it. Never mind, my mother told me to never go there. God would punish me for telling the truth, the whole truth, and nothing but the truth. She told me to stay out of it. The courts would handle it later. Anyway, at ten we got to start drinking a little of the wine. Don't ask why—it was just an altar-boy thing. After three or four belts of that stuff, the sermons actually sounded pretty good. Maybe that was why all the dads went out for a stiff one. It helped them get the word a little better—or maybe sleep through it.

One time I had a couple of sips too many. So did the fourteen-year-old boy with me. They had this little machine that made the hosts. You stuck a piece of bread in it. Then you pushed down on it, flattening the bread and cutting out four nice neat, round, little hockey pucks. At least that's what they looked like after too much cheap wine. When the priest came in the dressing room, expecting to have two little angels ready to lead the procession, he found two drunken children throwing little, round hosts all over the room. We must have gone through three loafs of some low-grade bread made by a bunch of monks in the mountains who hadn't spoken in years. Although it was only a nickel a loaf in those days, he was still mad. He had our fathers summoned immediately. The best part was watching the priest yelling at two drunken parents, with wine on his own breath, condemning two little boys to hell for stealing church wine and drinking it. I thought about offering to pee in a cup and give it back, but I knew I was in enough trouble as it was. Or was I? After church I was expecting the usual, which was getting the crap beat out of me in front of the other families so they all knew who the boss was in our house. Instead I got a hug. I think Dad was sort of proud of his chip off the old block. He always gave me a sip of his beer after that. He found another drinking buddy. The only rule was, "Don't tell Mom."

One year, the church was having a hard time financially. Contributions were way down. The parish priest was becoming very concerned. He was a nice-enough priest although his sermons were often close to an hour. After much deliberation and many failed fundraisers, the church board decided to offer him money for not speaking. Every five minutes he shaved off his lengthy Sunday sermons, each family would give an extra dollar. He began giving thirty-minute sermons and then fifteen-minute ones. In two years, the church received a major overhaul, a new parish hall was built, and four new classrooms were added on. They were all paid for in cash.

Shortly after that, he transferred to another church downtown. Right after he got there, someone broke into the church and stole some valuable church artifacts. As they were sneaking out with a bag of priceless items, this same priest was coming out of the shower and had nothing on except a towel. He saw the thief exiting the side door of the church and gave chase. He actually caught the guy and wrestled him to the ground. During the scuffle, his bath towel fell off. When the police arrived, they saw a guy naked, except for a white collar around his neck, lying on top of the thief. The thief was arrested for breaking and entering as well as burglary. The priest was questioned for public nudity and indecent exposure until the police figured out what had happened. Actually, he got his picture in the newspaper and was celebrated as a local hero.

In Catholic grade schools, we had to go to church every day. My teacher said it was God allowing us to be forgiven every day for our sins. I liked it because I got to sin more and did not have to go to hell. Our souls were black, they told us. We were dirty sinners, and an angry God stood watch over us every minute, waiting for us to screw up. Each time we did, another mark was scribed on a stonewall somewhere with our name on it: "Little Ronnie Weber, twelve sins this week." Then our black souls were changed to lily-white each time we went in the little confessional box. "Dear Father, I have sinned. My last confession was yesterday." I wonder if our souls ever got tired of being cleaned so many times. My shirts did. When they got really bad, we had to throw them away and get new ones. *Dear God, my soul had been washed so many times, it is yellow and green. I know I am only six, but can I have a new one? Can I give my Protestant friend, Steve, my old one? At least it's Catholic.* In the summer, we had to take catechism classes. There was no way they were going to let us off all summer. They didn't have enough priests for the fall rush. "Dear Father, I have sinned. My last confession was three months ago. I lied eight thousand seven hundred and twelve times. I had three thousand seven hundred and eighty-five dirty thoughts, and I stole four hundred thirty-two times." No, we got to go to church all summer long. Big Father was watching. I knew I had to go to confession a lot because I was an accident.

My second-grade teacher was six feet, two inches tall. She was also the school vice principal and disciplinarian. Her name was Sister Valerie Ann. The kids all respected her because she was so tall, she was closer to God. We also respected a large wooden ruler she had sitting on her desk. When I got in trouble and got the ruler across my knuckles, I was used to getting hit, and it didn't bother me much. The other kids told me to scream really loud. If you didn't, you might get hit some more. After that I always had my homework done on time. It was no use telling my mother I scraped my knuckles, falling on the sidewalk.

"What happened to your hands? Your knuckles are all red."

"Oh, nothin'."

"Sister Valerie Ann, huh?"

"Yep. Forgot to do my homework."

"Gosh, officious. You're always forgetting to do your homework. Don't you know you embarrass your parents when you get in trouble? You know that makes your father and I look bad. They will think we are bad parents. Ha ha ha."

I learned two things that day. The first was the word *officious*. I would hear that until her death seventy years later: "Gosh-officious this, gosh-officious that." I wondered what that word meant. No one would ever tell me, but when I heard it, I knew Mom was mad about something. When I grew up, I found it in a dictionary: "assertive of authority in an annoyingly domineering way, especially with regard to petty or trivial matters." The second thing I learned was another lesson on looking Catholic. It sure was a lot of work. In addition to always making sure people were looking at you pretending to be doing the right thing and pretending to be observing others pretending to be doing the right thing, you were never supposed to embarrass your parents. If they were supposed to be doing the right thing, then a child embarrassing them made them look bad. This was not allowed. Do that and you get the belt.

Then there was my Catholic high school. My first year was pretty quiet. My experience in grade school had been with not a single male priest teacher. We only had women nuns. In high school it was all male priests. They were big and a bit intimidating. They also carried sticks and paddles. They were also not afraid to use them. But by my second year I was back to my old attention-getting pranks again. That year, I tried to beat the world record for spats. Spats were a form of CBM, or Catholic behavior modification. However, they did not seem to work very well on me as I kept getting in trouble. I grabbed my ankles and took ten whacks somewhere between twenty and fifty times that year. Ouch! On my third year, the vice principal made a modification to the paddle. He had previously used a flattened-out baseball bat. Now he learned that by drilling lots of holes in the flat part, it would move faster through the air and hurt more. One time to the boy's bathroom with that thing and I decided I had felt enough CBM for a while.

If you ever meet me and you want to tell me something you are serious about, please don't use the terms, "swear to God." In decades gone by, we Catholics were always saying things like that or "on my mother's grave" while we were lying to you. In one of my later high school years, one of my teacher's name was Fr. Mulcahy. I was against the wall on the right-hand side of the class. On the other side was a solid wall of windows. We were in the middle of a midterm exam. I turned to my right and tried to whisper through my arm and armpit to the guy behind me. I said something like, "What did you answer for number six?" Apparently, I thought, since I couldn't see the teacher, he couldn't see me. This guy was built like a tank and six feet, four inches tall. He stood up and walked over to me. Sitting down and looking up at him made me feel like I was talking to the Jolly Green Giant. When he asked me if I was cheating, I denied the whole thing, saying, "No, sir, swear to God." He walked back to his desk and sat down. About ten minutes later, when he could see I was done with the rest of the test, he walked back over and towered over me, saying, "Remember, Mr. Weber, you swore to God." His eyes bored right through me. I think I peed in my pants. I still shiver every time I think of that day. Those guys could really scare you. Father Mulcahy, if you are still out there, I am sorry I lied. Please don't tell the vice principal about it. I am older and arthritic now. It would be almost impossible for me to bend over and grab my ankles. Besides, I have osteoporosis. If he hit me with that new-styled paddle, he would probably break my butt.

When I got married, my wife's parents were deathly afraid of Catholics. They lived in New Jersey, not far from New York City. They told us that back there, Catholics were mobsters. They didn't like me. My mother refused to let me marry anyone other than a Catholic. So we ran away and eloped. Sometime later, we finally did have a real wedding. It was held in a Catholic church, presided over by both a Catholic priest and a Presbyterian minister. My wife was a secretary in a bank and would later become a grade-school teacher. I was sort of a hood and owned a motorcycle shop. No one gave us a chance to make it. That was in 1973, and we are still together. Go figure.

Then there was this priest who married me and my beautiful wife. This guy rode a motorcycle and taught in a Catholic high school. He was so damn good-looking. I gave him two years before he left the priesthood. I missed it by one. Not too long after he wedded us, I saw him at a grocery store in Levi's and a T-shirt. Alongside of him was a beautiful young blonde holding a newborn baby. When he saw me, his face turned a bit pink although there was a smile on his face. No words were spoken from either of us. They didn't have to be. I noticed a wedding band on him. He grinned all the way out the door. We both chuckled. I never saw him again. I hope God forgave him.

FRECKLES

I remember our car trips to the mountains. We had these two big cars for many years. They had only two doors and no roll-down windows in the back. Mom and Dad would sit up front and puff, puff, puff. The four of us—Richard, Robert, Rosalind, and Ronald—were lined up according to age and size in the back seat. On long trips it got hard to see who was where because of the big cloud of smoke inside the car. The only time we got fresh air was when Dad rolled down the window to throw an empty beer bottle out the window. We would try to hold our breaths between window roll downs, but never could seem to make it. Sometimes he drank so fast, we got close though. His favorite place was a small mountain town named Rhododendron, Oregon. It was near Mount Hood. My mom said it was his favorite because there was a bar less than a hundred feet from cabin number 2 at the Zigzag Motel. Mom said it was called the Zigzag Motel because it was on the curvy Rhododendron River. We thought it was called Zigzag because that's how Dad drove going there. He would zig and throw an empty beer bottle and then zag back on the road. Rick said Dad liked it there because the river ran fifteen feet from the cabin. When he got sick from drinking too much, he could run just a few feet and feed the fish. Dad was really nice. A lot of fish were alive because of him.

Growing up was fun sometimes. We got to join a fancy club. Mom said we had a lot of money because Dad got a lot of people drunk and sold them life insurance. Now we had two new cars and a huge house with live-in help. I found out later, the live-in help was there because they were alive in the morning. My parents didn't have a heartbeat until around noon in those days. Someone had to get us fed, dressed, and off to school in the morning, so that job belonged to Mrs. Dolan. The fancy club was called the Multnomah Athletic Club. If you were rich and liked to drink a lot, this was the place to be. Times were good. We won the big war (WWII). This club was a haven for us. It had everything. When I was a child, I was on the ski team, the boxing team, the swimming team, and a few other things. I wanted to join the running club so I could learn how to run away from my father. Unfortunately, they didn't have a running club. I thought the boxing club might help, but I was only eight. It would be a long time before I could box his ears. He and Mom were always saying that: "I'm gonna box your ears." The choice was a tough one: Go to the club, or go home and get hit or yelled at. We went to the club every day sometimes. It was an easy bus ride from school. They even had a few rooms on the top floor where people could live. There was about a half dozen or so beautiful apartments. I asked Faye at the front desk if I could live there. Faye worked at the front desk for over forty years. She was really nice to us and funny. I wondered if she would like a nice little Irish boy with red hair and freckles. I could mow her lawn. She told me I couldn't live at the club. The apartments were for old people. Actually, some of them were for people who drank too much and couldn't get home that night.

"Ha ha ha, you're funny, Ronnie. Go find your parents now."

"Where are they? I haven't seen them in over five hours."

"They're in the bar. Run along now. Go swimming."

My parents brought us there a lot. It was like the best place in the world. We could swim, run on an indoor track, lift weights, wrestle, and do much more. There was even a boxing room. The MAC club, as it was called, was also a haven for my parents too. There were fancy dining rooms, bars, nightclubs, and the works. They could go drink and complain about everything, then eat and go dancing, all in the same night.

"Where are the kids, June?"

"Who cares? Would you like another drink? How about dinner? There is a great band here tonight. Let's stay for the music and dancing. Light my cigarette for me, honey, people are watching. Ha ha ha."

There were four of us kids, Richard, Robert, Rosalind, and Ronald. Our parents called us Ricky, Bobby, Lyn, and Ronnie. At the MAC club they had a huge PA system with speakers all over the club. Sometimes when our parents needed us, they would go to Faye at the front desk and page us.

"Ricky Weber to the front desk, please. Ricky Weber to the front desk, please."

"Hi, Faye."

"Hi, honey. Listen, Ricky. Your folks are going to stay in the bar for a while. You guys go to the dining room, and get whatever you want to eat."

Richard, Robert, Rosalind, and Ronald marched off to the dining room, per Dad's instructions to Faye. *I wish Rick would beat him up. I want to go home. The Lone Ranger is on TV tonight.* Having money had its advantages. We had one of the first TVs in the neighborhood. It was the neatest thing on earth in the early 1950s.

We made it home that night, zigging and zagging all the way up Canyon Road. Dad and Mom had all the windows rolled up and were both smoking like chimney stacks. *God, please let Dad open up a window and throw an empty beer bottle out. I feel like I have to feed the fish.* When we got home, Dad went straight to the basement. Our basement was huge, with a four-stool bar, a large dance floor, and a small spot in one corner for a band. My parents entertained down there a lot. I guess it was easier to sell insurance if you got them all drunk at your house. The basement and bar were done in sort of a Polynesian style. My father served time in the South Pacific with the merchant marines. He somehow was stuck back in time in that place. He would play the record album *South Pacific* over and over for many years. He would sit down there in the quiet and dark, by the fire, lost in the South Pacific, with the beautiful Polynesian women, sipping his drinks and smoking his cigarettes.

When he was down there, we were not allowed to make a sound. He loved turning off all the lights, eating pills, drinking, smoking, sitting by the fire, and listening to his soft music. If one of us walked around upstairs and he heard footsteps or the floor creak, it was the belt. One time, I was supposed to take his dinner downstairs to him. It was about 9:00 p.m. I was desperately trying to carry a heavy plate of meat loaf, gravy, and potatoes down the staircase to the basement. There were exactly fourteen steps. I remember it well, running from him a few times when he was mad. This particular time, I spilled a little gravy on one of the steps. He hated messes. Even one drop of water on the floor or one grain of rice spilled while eating dinner, and it was curtains for the guilty one. I leaned a little to see the gravy spill, hoping he wouldn't notice. I would clean it up quickly on the way back up. However, I leaned too far, and everything went bouncing down the stairs—meat, gravy, and potatoes. Running from him was easy. He was usually too drunk to catch you. The trick was, would he remember it all the next day? If he did, you would wish you took the licking last night. So I stayed that night and took it. Ouch! A few months later, I got even with him. He was mad about something and came tearing out of the house, yelling my name. He was really drunk, and I knew he might eventually catch me, so I started running around the car as fast as I could. About five times around that big car, and he was so dizzy, he fell down, threw up, and passed out. One of the neighbor kids told me I was going to die the next day. Dad would remember it all and kill me. I told him that at least I'd get to go to heaven. He was Protestant, and our priest said he had to go to hell. I was keeping some of my dirty yellow-and-green souls in the closet for some other kids, not him. If they took a dirty Catholic soul with them when they died, they could go to purgatory for a while and then to heaven. The kid told me to go to hell and ran away. Luckily, the next day, my dad didn't remember a thing. Now he drank all night long too. He said even the phenobarbital didn't work. So now he had to drink twenty-four hours a day. He said it was Mom's fault and hit her again.

One of our best hiding places was in the woods. Behind our house, there were around twenty-five acres of thick, dense forest. We built forts and played games our whole life growing up. One summer, we decided to build underground forts. Kids from blocks away came every day. We had twenty or more kids helping. We would start early in the morning and continue until it got dark. Mothers made lunches, and fathers came after work to see the progress. It was a long, steep climb down to an area we called the first creek and then a steep climb back up to a flatland before the second creek. Our forts were in between the two creeks. Someone who had a couple of drinks under their belt could not make this trek. My father never saw our forts. If we tried to do something like that today, every environmental agency west of the Mississippi would shut us down. We had a steep incline into the main fort. There was a living room on the main level and then another steep incline down to a lower level that we called the bedroom. This was all underground. Tons of dirt had to be removed for this, and it was a miracle it didn't collapse and kill all of us. We loved it so because it was hiding from Dad. We started in June and finished in September, about the time we had to go back to school. Once it was done, it wasn't really that great. It was just building it that was so much fun. One of my favorite things was to go down to the first level and wait in the dark. I would blow out all the candles and turn out the flashlights. I used to pretend my father finally came out to see what we were doing. I sat there waiting with a baseball bat and big rock.

"Hi, Dad. Come on down, and see what we built. Look over there, Dad." *Smack!* In my mind's eye, I knocked him out with a baseball bat and buried him under a ton of dirt. Then I imagined what I would tell Mom.

"Hey, Mom, I just hit Dad over the head with a baseball bat and a rock. I buried him in the underground fort."

"Oh, that's nice, honey. Where's my cigarettes? Get me an ashtray, would you please."

Fortunately, one of the parents finally realized how unsafe the fort was, and it was shut down before it collapsed and buried a couple of us alive.

Another escape was to a place called Camp Silver Creek. It was a Catholic summer camp about an hour from Portland. We would go every summer for many years. My first summer there, I got really homesick one night. Bob was in a cabin in another part of the camp. When I told him about it, he made this funny face and reminded me of dad and his belt. I stopped being homesick. We did everything in that camp. We swam, shot bow and arrows, went in rowboats, hiked, fished, had campfires, and so much more. I remember being really shy a lot. Then one year they told me the counselors wouldn't hit me, and I started having a lot more fun. The last year I was there, my mother showed me another one of her tricks. We were driving down about a ten-mile stretch of road, and she started driving really fast. When she dropped her cigarette, I thought that was kind of weird. She never dropped three things—a drink, a cigarette, or the telephone. They were always in her hand. I kept hearing *hiss, hiss, hiss.*

"Mom, what's wrong? Why are you driving so fast?"

"Shut up and get on the floor. *Now!*"

I crawled down under the dashboard and tried not to cry. All I could hear was *hiss, hiss, hiss,* and I saw her feet moving up and down real fast on the pedals, especially the big one in the middle. It was called the brake pedal. I really wanted to hear her fake little laugh more than ever right now. Ha ha ha. But it wasn't there. I looked up, and her hands were moving wildly around the steering wheel. Her bony, little, arthritic fingers were wrapped like barbwire around the steering wheel. I thought I saw blood. Her face was white as a sheet, and the car was bouncing all over the road. The tires were screeching, and dust was flying everywhere. When I heard, "Our father in heaven…," I knew we were in trouble.

Fifteen minutes later, we were in a gas station surrounded by a police car and some curious onlookers. There were blackberry vines underneath the car and scratches down the side. My mom was on the pay phone with a cigarette in her hand. I stayed under the dashboard awhile, afraid to move. Finally, I was able to sit up and see all the people. Several of them will talking really fast.

"That lady came all the way down that mountain with no brakes. I don't know how she didn't crash."

"She must have been going seventy miles an hour around those hairpin turns. They oughtta be dead."

From inside the phone booth, I heard "Ha ha ha" and could see that fake Irish smile again. I think for the first time, I was really glad to see it. Maybe she could be my mom after all. Now I only had to find a different dad.

"Gosh, officious, what's everyone so upset about? It was fun, like a roller-coaster ride, right, honey?"

"Yeah, right, Mom."

A pint of brake fluid, a couple of tightened bolts, and we were back on the road again. She never once admitted to me being scared. We never talked about it again. Just typing this out gives me the chills and draws up a few tears. My mother was really one strong lady.

Another great escape was our grandpa Tony's house. His first wife's name was Alice Dempsey. She had died from some of those big words—*alcoholism* and *emphysema*. She was fifty-four years old. Her father was a famous boxer. His name was Jack Dempsey. I learned a lot about him later. He was the middleweight champion of the world and died around the turn of the century. He fought mostly during the 1890s. Later, around 1925, another fighter named William Harrison Dempsey changed his first name to Jack in honor of my great-grandfather. He became the world heavyweight champion. Over the years, many people mistook them for the same person. Grampa Dempsey died of tuberculosis. He was in his thirties when he died. My grandfather Tony married again after the death of Grandma Alice. This time, Grandpa Tony married a really nice lady named Bess. This was before I was born, so Bess was the only grandmother I would ever know on that side of the family. They had this huge home. We could play hide-and-seek all over it. However, we had to be careful about the basement. Grandma said there were "girly" magazines down there. I found one once. Yuck! We were not supposed to look in the drawers. Grandma said there were whiskey bottles and cigars in there. We were too young for that stuff. Grandpa spent a lot of time down there. He always had a smile on his face and stunk like cigars when he came up from the basement. I wonder why. He lived until he was ninety-three. Good Grandpa.

Grandma and Grandpa never hit us. They always had warm big smiles and huge meals. The home was always a warm and happy place. Grandma gave great hugs and even better birthday and Christmas presents. I think they always felt bad about Dad. The only time I saw Grandpa cry was at my father's funeral. Mom said it was hard to bury a child. Grandpa had to bury his only son. His little boy was fifty-four. Grandpa was eighty. Poor Grandpa.

The Bees

On a hot July day in 1958, when I was ten years old, I was playing in the woods with some friends. I accidentally stepped on a hole that was an underground beehive. The hole gave way, and I got stung by a bee. When I jumped back, yellow jackets poured out of the hole by the hundreds, angry and stinging. My friends took off running as fast as they could. With bees swarming around my body and stinging me, I started running toward my house, yelling for my parents to help. I could see my friends running ahead of me. All I could do was pray. I kept saying, "God, help us, God, help us." Then I just started screaming and crying, feeling one sting after another. By the time I got home, the swarm was gone, but I had been stung fifty or more times. I will always remember lying in the bathtub, counting all the red sores. I survived the incident. However, the doctor said I would be very allergic to beestings for the rest of my life. A single beesting could cost me my life.

Twelve years later, in November of 1970, I was working in a neighbor's yard. Suddenly, I saw a small, black cloud over the house, like a puff of black smoke. The cloud moved quickly toward the ground. I heard some screams and saw a small boy, about six, running across the yard. The boy had been stung two or three times and was trying to get into the house. "Mommy, Mommy," he cried as his mother and a neighbor looked on, frozen by fear. The black cloud was a huge swarm of bees. Someone had burned some paper and other debris in the fireplace. It was the first time since the prior winter that anything had been burned in that fireplace. Over the summer, a nest of bees had been built just inside the chimney, near the top. When the smoke and flames worked their way up the chimney, thousands of mad bees swarmed out of there. I was twenty-two years old and in good physical shape. I had just finished a three-year tour with the US Army. "God, help us," I said and ran toward the child. I grabbed him up and raced quickly into the house. Witnesses said the huge, black cloud of bees were less than ten feet from the boy when I grabbed him. The bees smashed into the front door as the mother quickly slammed it shut. With my allergy to bees, I was very lucky I did not get stung. I ignored the doctor's warning about beestings and trusted in God to help save the boy from a lot of bee stings. If that cloud of bees had caught up with him, he could have died. Sometimes faith is just knowing God will be there when you need him most.

Fifteen years later, in 1985, I was thirty-seven years old, happily married, and the father of two young boys. We were camping at Detroit Lake in Central Oregon. A large group of us were sitting around a table, talking and playing cards, when I heard some screams. I told everyone to be quiet as I heard a child yelling and sensed trouble. The others at the table told me it was just some kids playing. For as long as I live, I will never forget my reply. I shouted out, "I know terror when I hear it. Somewhere there is a child in trouble!" The table fell silent with startled faces staring at me in shock. I jumped to my feet and ran in the direction of the child's voice. I ran over fifty yards up a hill and down through the woods. When I came out of the trees to a clearing, I actually knocked a person down, trying to get through a crowd of onlookers. On the ground was a child screaming and rolling around. He or she was covered with bees. There were so many bees, you could not even tell if the child was a boy or girl. Once again, I uttered, "God, help us," quickly swooped up the child, and ran toward the lake. I am sure the water was only a few feet away, but it seemed like one of those slow-motion dreams where you were trying to run, and your legs moved really slow. The child (later we would find out it was a young boy) had been playing in the woods and had knocked down a large beehive. When it hit the ground, it broke, and the bees swarmed the child. As I was running toward the water, with this poor child covered in bees and screaming, the bees started to engulf me too. They were stinging me all over. They covered my hands, arms, legs, and face. They were getting all tangled up in my then long hair and stinging the top of my head. I continued to pray as I ran, "God, help the both of us." I was exhausted. Just when I was ready to collapse, something seemed to help me in the last few yards. I felt like an angel gave me one little extra push when I needed it the most. When I arrived at the water, I jumped in, still holding the boy. Once in the water, I started wiping the bees off the child and myself. The more I wiped, the more they stung. The only thing I could do was completely submerge myself and the child. A few seconds underwater and the bees were rendered helpless. As I didn't have time to take a deep breath or warn the boy what I was going to do, we just went straight under the water. We both came up choking on water and gasping for air. While it seemed like an eternity, the entire affair lasted only a minute or two. As we were way up in the woods and over an hour from a hospital, the two of us were taken to a small-town doctor nearby. The boy almost died. I should have.

The following day I was allowed to see the little boy for a few minutes. Although he was scared and very sick, the doctor said he would recover just fine. The doctor then looked at me and said, "It's a good thing neither of you are allergic to bees." I told the doctor what had happened twenty-seven years before and said that I was, in fact, deathly allergic to bees. The doctor examined me, and although I was stung several dozen times, I was fine. I was not even sick. The doctor tried to give medical explanations about people doing spectacular things during adrenaline rushes, like soldiers in combat and that sort of thing, but he had no explanation for this. There was not a mark on me. By all rights, I should have died moments after all those stings. Only something divine could have been behind what happened that day.

Dad

Seven years before the death of my father, I came home from school and found a Multnomah County sheriff talking quietly to Mom in the living room. I was nine, almost ten. Mom was signing some papers. Dad never came home again after that day. He drove by the house occasionally, visiting neighbors, but he never came to the house. A few years later, I would learn some more big words, like restraining order, wife beating, and child abuse. He disappeared for seven years, living in a small mountain cabin in the woods. It was at his favorite place, Rhododendron. Now he had to drink alone and had no one to hit. Poor Dad. I saw him once at the cabin for about fifteen minutes when I was fourteen. My brother Bob and I went skiing at Mount Hood. Bob wanted to see where he lived. It was a very short, uncomfortable visit. He gave me a bowl of cereal to eat. When he went to the bathroom, I threw it—milk and all—behind the couch. I knew it would be days before he found it, and only the rotten smell of spoiled milk would lead him to it. Ha ha ha. Bob said he couldn't come and get me back because of the restraining order. If he did, I could have him put in jail. Come on, Dad, put 'em up.

I saw him for the last time four years later. The visit only lasted about a minute or two. I was told he was in a nursing home in the area. I had just gotten my driver's license and decided to go see him. The nurse told me he was in a room down the hall. There was only an old guy, about ninety, sitting in the room. I went back to the nurse's station and informed them they had sent me to the wrong room. They told me that Mr. Weber was, in fact, in that room and walked me back there. On the way, the woman told me he was dying of lung cancer and alcoholism. *Haven't I heard those words somewhere before?* When we entered the room, her words seemed distant, like in some kind of dream.

"Mr. Weber, you have a visitor." She promptly left.

The next discussion would remain with me until my death. It stays there like an old movie rerun. His head turned slowly toward me, and a fake smile appeared on his face. It seemed like it took a whole minute. Looking up at me with those sad, puppy-dog eyes he always had, he froze up like a cold statue. I didn't know whether to slug him in the face, leave, or stand there and cry.

"Are you Mr. Weber?" My voice trembled. I could not call him Dad. There suddenly was too much anger. Besides, this guy now seemed over a hundred. My dad was fifty-four.

"Yes," a hoarse, raspy old voice came back to me.

"Do you know who I am?"

"Are you Ronnie?"

"Yes."

I still couldn't call him Dad, and he didn't dare use the word *son.* Too much had happened. There was so much I wanted to say, but I couldn't. He just sat there with a drink and a cigarette, looking like a little boy who was ashamed of himself. He looked like he had been caught doing something wrong. Back in those days, people who were dying were allowed to drink and smoke in nursing homes. It made no difference now. His eyes stayed on the floor after he first looked at me. The shame hung in the room like heavy living-room drapes. The nurse returned to the room and told me to come back in the morning. His medications made him dopey in the evening, and he needed to go to bed. I left without shaking the hand that had hit all of us so many times. I couldn't touch him. Not another word was spoken by either of us. It was too late. The damage was done. He turned away from me and stared at the wall. I turned and walked out.

The following morning, the phone rang early in the morning. It always did during the week. My mother was a substitute teacher and got calls daily. The conversation was always the same.

"Hello… Uh-huh, uh-huh, uh-huh. Thank you. Goodbye."

I thought it was the Portland School District substitute hotline telling my mother to drive ten or twenty miles away and teach something like sophomore American literature or whatever else was needed that day. As a substitute teacher, every day it was something different. She liked that. At five feet tall and a whopping ninety pounds, she could handle the toughest class in the toughest high school in Portland. Her red Irish hair and temper were well-known around the school district. Getting beat for seventeen years by her husband and raising four kids alone made her tough. My bedroom was right next to hers, and when the phone rang in the morning, it was my job to get her up.

"Come on, Mom, get up. You gotta go to work, and bring home the dough."

She always liked me doing that. She liked using the expression "bringing home the dough." When she didn't get up, I insisted and heard something that would stay with me until I die.

"Mom, come on, get up. You have to go teach."

"No, honey, that wasn't the school district. It was the nursing home. Your father died. Go back to bed."

My mother turned on her side, pulled up the covers, and went back to sleep. I went to my bedroom and just sat on the bed. I was confused. I mean, I hated the bastard. I had wished him dead for years for all the abuse. I had unfinished business with him. There was a lot I wanted to say to him. I wanted to really tell him off for all the drinking, smoking in the car, hitting, spanking, never showing up to ball games, and so much more. I also wanted to beat the crap out of him. I knew then, at seventeen years old, I would never get a chance. He was dead.

My mom, who had not seen or spoken to my father for seven years, decided to have a funeral for him. When I walked past his open casket, I spit on him. You heard me right. I guess it was all that deep-seated anger that made me do it. Spitting on his casket was just my way of paying him back. To make things even stranger, when my mother was dying, she wanted to be laid to rest next to the man who had hurt all of us. She said that he was her lawfully wedded husband as they had never divorced. Today they still lie side by side in the Mount Calvary Cemetery in Portland. Go figure.

Forgiveness

I have a picture that someone took of my father about a month before he passed away. He was six-feet-one-inch tall and weighed eighty pounds. He looked like the living dead. I often wanted to toss it out, but I kept it. Today I look at it maybe once a year. The picture helps me continue to have compassion for the poor guy. In my seventies I have a wonderful wife, kids, and grandkids whom only a loving God could make. My health is fantastic. I hike continuously and occasionally still climb a mountain. I spend most of my days, eating my wife's wonderful cooking, doing volunteer work, writing, hiking, and fussing over the grandkids. One of my favorite hobbies is doing tai chi in a deep forest in the middle of the night. In the darkness my only audience is a few owls or maybe an early-rising deer. I love to watch the deer as the sun rises, and they just stand there watching me pretend I am Bruce Lee. They do not clap when I am done—rather, they just meandered off into a thicket of Douglas fir trees. If deer laugh, they probably are howling at my performance. In short, I have been given all the happiness and joy a human being could possibly receive. My dad missed out on so much happiness. I feel sad for him. The anger is gone, and the compassion is still there. I hope there is a heaven, and he is in it. God knows he suffered enough on this earth.

Despite all that had happened, I do have a few good memories of him. I cherish them as living proof that before the booze, he really was a good guy. One memory is of him tossing me up and down in the air, making these funny noises that I cannot describe in writing. Sometimes he would call me Sputnik after the Russian satellite as I was this little, freckle-faced kid with red hair and so full of energy. I was always running around the house and yard like a satellite in orbit. I also remember trips to the mountains and to the beach. We would rent cabins. Our days were full of adventure (often as our parents were sleeping it off after partying the night before). Then at night they were drinking and dancing the night away at some nightclub once again. Thus, we had lots of time to explore the mountains, beaches, and anything else we could find. These are good memories, and I still have them. Although a child should have more than just a few good memories of a parent, I will take what I can get. It was more than some kids got. Sadly, for my father, the magic in alcohol was gone. Mom was able to quit, but Dad wasn't so lucky. Our family doctor started prescribing phenobarbital to help with sleep and something else to help with the morning jitters. Soon came three attempts to recover at the Raleigh Hills Treatment Center in Southwest Portland. All three attempts failed, and he would eventually die way too early.

In the end I had to forgive him in order to move on with my life. The forgiveness started one night as I was with a group of friends, complaining about my father once again. I could see the faces looking back at me that projected a familiar look. Their expressions silently shouted out a chorus, *Oh god, not this story again.*

One evening, my friend Jim asked me when I was going to quit whining about my father. He reminded me that I was almost sixty years old and needed to let it go. He was right. I had been a victim long enough. After some counseling and a lot of soul-searching, I was musing it over with a firm resolve to do something about it. I just didn't know what to do or how to do it. I prayed and waited.

On Veterans Day 2008 I drove past a local park where a group of former soldiers were holding a ceremony. I stopped to observe. After it was over, I walked around the park and noticed a bunch of newly laid bricks. Some had names on them, and a couple were blank. A WWII veteran walked up beside me and asked me if I was a veteran. I told him yes, and he asked me to consider buying a brick to help support the park. It seemed like a nice thing to do, so I said yes. For about a year or two after the brick was inscribed, I would stop in and look at it on a regular basis. I would stand there, reading my name and reminiscing about my military service. There had only been two empty spots in that particular area of bricks, and I had bought one of them. The remaining blank brick was down one row and on the left. They touched in one corner. That brick stayed blank for nearly two years, and it was bothering me for some reason, sort of like unfinished business. I thought about buying it and then donating it to someone so it would have a name on it. It was always just a passing thought.

Months later, I saw Jim around town. We sat down and talked a bit as people often did. Upon our parting he looked at me and said, "So have you forgiven your dad yet?"

I told him that I had. However, he was a wise old guy and could see some reservation on my part. He asked me specifically what I had done to forgive my father. I had written a letter to my deceased father. Jim had instructed me to do that a few months back. I apologized to my father for anything I had done to make him mad. I was very hyper as a child, and sometimes my dad would blow up about it. I told him that I loved him and that I forgave him. The letter had helped, but Jim could see that I was still a bit stuck. I still had some anger about it. I had previously read the letter out loud to Jim, as that was part of the process. But now I had to do one more thing. I sat quietly with thinking before I would answer him. Sometimes thoughts slowly ease into our heads, and other times they just pop in. Suddenly, it all came clear—the brick. I told Jim that I would like to buy a brick at that park where my brick was. He agreed. I drove straight to the memorial park and ran to my brick, hoping the one next to it was still blank. It was. I bought the brick, and a few weeks later I received a call that it had been inscribed. I drove right down there to see it. My stomach was filled with butterflies, and I was not sure why. I guess I was just nervous and excited at the same time. There our bricks were, touching each other at one corner. When I stood in front of that brick and read the words, I fell down to my knees and cried.

ROBERT E. WEBER   RON WEBER U.S. ARMY

MERCHANT MARINES   KOREAN DMZ 1967–1969

HUSBAND AND FATHER   AGENT ORANGE

A man I had hated all my life was now sitting beside me on a veterans' memorial wall in Beaverton, Oregon. I had grown into a man myself and had made many mistakes too. I vividly remember my voice cracking between the sobbing. *Who the hell am I to hate someone for so long when I am far from perfect myself?*

I am sure my mother was right. He was a great guy before the booze got him. The older kids in my family remembered some of the good times. It was just my luck that, as the youngest child, I would not see much of them. Regardless of the past, I was now free to stop the hate. My forgiveness of my father was complete. I have felt no malice toward him since that day many years ago.

Mom

A short time after high school, I joined the United States Army. All of us had left to be married, go in the service, or go to college in a very short time. I remember Mom telling me that she was relieved we were all gone. She had no strength or money left. When my father left, I was ten years old. All that money was gone. We didn't even have a car. We all somehow had to make it on our own now. She was just plain worn-out. Even the "ha ha ha" was gone. Three years later, I came back from the army. Mom was alone now and had been all that time. She had sold the huge family home and moved to a tiny house across the street from the church and school we grew up in. She asked me to stay for a while. I was going to go to school and could use a place to live. It would work out fine. I think she was really lonely now and could appreciate the company. There she sat at the dining-room table every night with her books. Substituting school for a bunch of ungrateful high school kids had finally gotten to her. She was going back to school to get her master's. She was fifty-five years old. Night after night, we studied together in that tiny house. I didn't want to go to school; however, if she could do it at almost retirement age, by god, so could I. During those few years together as adults, I finally got to know her in a way I never had before. I am glad she was my mom. She had worked really hard to keep us all in good Catholic schools. All four of us went to college and had great careers. Our mom made that happen, and we have never forgotten that. After she received her master's degree, she got a job as a department head in the English Department at the University of Portland, a prestigious Catholic college in Oregon. She stayed there until she retired fifteen years later at the age of seventy.

My mother bought a small house in walking distance from the college. She was finally happy, and it was wonderful to see that. Then something else happened that still makes me laugh. I was married now and starting a family with my wife, Lydia. One day I went over to her house, and there was a man working in the yard. Mom and the gardener were laughing and having a good time. I was shocked. This hard Irish woman who had been through hell and back was actually enjoying the company of a man. However, I soon found out that he wasn't the gardener.

"Hi, honey," Mom said with a big smile.

"I want you to meet Joe."

I walked over and shook Joe's hand. He was a handsome big man with a strong grip and a huge smile—a real nice guy. I was just shocked and happy for her. *Thank you, God.* Then my mom dropped the bomb.

"Father Joe works at the university with me."

Father Joe? OMG. The guy is a Catholic priest? As it would turn out, they would become best friends for nearly twenty years before his death. He would come to her house for dinner every Sunday. He mowed the lawn and worked in the garden right alongside her year after year. I wonder what else they did. Ha ha ha. God seemed to close the eyes of the church on that one. Everyone who worked in the college and the students knew they were together a lot; however, no one seemed to care. They were so happy together, even God let it slide by. The strangest part of it all was that my mother was a Catholic nun right out of college. She developed some serious health problems and had to leave the religious order. She would rarely talk about it. I think being Catholic all her life, teaching at a Catholic college, and having a Catholic priest as a best friend sort of made her feel good about the whole thing. And she finally found true love, something that she did not experience when she was married to my father. The last twenty years of her life were full of rich love and happiness—a job she worked hard for and got, a best friend, four successful children, and a handful of grandchildren. Ha ha ha.

Green Beans

Growing up, we had a live-in nanny named Mrs. Dolan. She lived in a bedroom that was down a hall where the garage used to be. It was a nice big room with her own bathroom. Our parents had a new double garage built off to the side of the house and down a hill a bit. The garage was wide and deep. Up above the garage was a huge room that was turned into a studio apartment. It was just one big space with a kitchen, an open living room, and an area in a corner for a bed. Behind the open room was a large closet on one side and a bathroom on the other side. The rear of the apartment had two huge windows with a fireplace in the middle. The view out the windows was a stunning forest that went on forever. That woods would be our playground until we left for college or the military. Even in the wet and cold winter, we were out there. Dad would come home from work, and if we were in the house, he would kick us out. So we built forts, played games, and fulfilled our fantasies. My favorite was running through the woods with a red cape, pretending to be Superman. It was even more fun on a bicycle because the cape would flap in the wind.

My mom liked to buy these awful S&W Green Beans. They came in a green can and tasted terrible. If we didn't eat the food that

Mrs. Dolan cooked, there would be consequences. My dad would stand by the dinner table and slap the shit out of us if we did not eat our vegetables. Like all kids, I was told that some starving child in China or Africa would be happy to eat those vegetables as they had no food to complain about in the first place. I would cry and eat the other food on the plate. Dad, yelling and hitting (open hand, closed fist, or belt), would force me to eat the damn things. Gagging, I tried not to throw up, or I was in big trouble. We four kids ate at a normal time while Mom and Dad ate later in the evening. That gave him more time to stand there and make sure I ate my vegetables. *Thanks, Dad. Why don't you go away?*

One day I was crying after getting spanked, and my brother Bob told me something that still resonates in my head seven decades later.

He said, "Why don't you eat the green beans first? Just stuff them in your mouth really fast, and then flush them down with some milk. Then eat something you like. Quickly shove some potatoes or meat down your throat to cover the awful taste. Then the bad stuff is gone, and you can enjoy all the other good food on the plate."

Thanks, Bob. What a great idea. I was only about five or six at the time, but I never forgot that. I also hated a few other vegetables like brussels sprouts, overcooked carrots, broccoli, and anything else green. I just did that green-bean thing, as I called it, for anything I didn't like—swallow the crap first, and move on to the good stuff. Seeing this, my dad quit hanging around the dinner table when the four of us kids ate dinner. He had to put his belt away and find something else to do besides whacking his kids over dinner. Bob was the wise one of us. Lyn was my protector and best friend. Rick was the busy one. He was my hero. I always looked up to him. Rick was six years older than me and was often gone somewhere with his friends. Sometimes all the neighborhood kids would be out in that woods. During the summer we went out there after dinner. But I had to eat my green   beans first.

Years later I was sitting in a mess hall at Camp Casey in Korea and minding my own business while eating dinner. Suddenly, I heard a loud voice from another table.

"Why do you do that?"

I turned to see who it was and what he was talking about. I just stared at him stupidly, and he spoke again.

"You always eat one thing at a time. You eat your vegetables first and then everything else afterward. Why do you do that?"

I proceeded to tell him the green-bean story, and we all had a good laugh. I am in my seventies, and I still eat the green stuff first—even if I like it, which I usually do.

Long after that time, I was sulking at work. It was a Monday, and I was hungover. My boss had given me a really crummy assignment, and I didn't want to do it. It was some daily reporting of what had gone on the day before at work. It had to be done daily. I would moan about it all day and finally get it done about a half hour before my workday was over. A lady comanager saw me and came over to see what was up. I told her, and she said, "Why don't you suck it up and just buzz through it right away when you come in the door first thing in the morning? Then you can do other more fun things throughout the day."

Bang. There it was—the green-bean theory. Fifty years later I was still doing it. Life is full of both fun things and stuff that is not so fun. Sitting around, stewing about something is so nonproductive. Get it over with, and move on. Eat those green beans of life, and enjoy the rest of the good stuff. I run into this every day. There is always someone who upsets me or something that breaks down. Maybe the weather went from warm and sunny to cold and rainy. Maybe your boss got after you, or traffic sucked. One of my favorites is how to handle disappointment in general. I really work fast to get through it. A super good example is a ticket. You are driving home after work, and you had a bad day. You're not paying attention, and you get a ticket. Maybe it was speeding or a red light. Sometimes it seems like there is nothing worse in this whole world than a ticket, except maybe cancer. I mean, everyone hates getting pulled over or getting caught by those damned cameras at a stoplight. I haven't had a ticket for many years; however, when I did, I would just swallow the vegetables and pay for it as soon as possible. That way it is not hanging over your head. Eat your green beans.

CHAPTER 3

KEEPING UP WITH THE FAMILY ALCOHOLIC TRADITION

Alcoholism is a great disease—to look back on, I mean. Actually, it was kind of fun for a while. I really enjoyed it until the red button broke—the one that says Stop. Actually, the green button for Go broke too. It got tired of being pushed all the time and melted.

"Please, God, get me through this, and I *swear*, I will *never* drink again as long as I live."

My favorite was, "I swear to you, God, I am not lying. Please don't make me throw up again (as though it were *his* fault). I will go to church every day of my life. I swear. I'll help children, read the Bible, and stop calling my boss an asshole (at least for a while). Please don't make me throw up again."

The drive to work sucked, especially on Monday mornings, but the ride home with a six-pack was much better. People at work often wondered why I was such an ass on Monday mornings and so happy on Fridays. I usually kept my promise on Mondays. I wouldn't drink. The day was so horrible, I can't imagine what my productivity looked like. The worst part was that me, the funniest guy in the world and the guy who talked so much, no one else could get a word in edgewise, was suddenly like the Buddha. I mean, there wasn't a sound out of me. I don't think I ever spoke a word on Monday mornings for ten years. After work, I would go straight home, take a bath, eat dinner, and go right to bed, usually around 6:30 to 7:00 p.m., telling my wife I was tired from all the yard work I did over the weekend. On Tuesdays, I began to speak inaudible sounds. Wednesday, I was perking up a little. By noon, I was jabbering a little. Still sober, I seemed to be alive again. Usually, after work on Wednesdays, the promise would get broken again. My wife had spent many years singing with a local jazz group. As they always practiced on Wednesday evenings, I could sneak a few beers in. I would go by the bar for one beer. Sometimes, the words *a couple* would appear. Whenever you ask a drunken alcoholic how many he or she had, it is always, "just a couple." That means we really don't want you to know, or we forgot entirely. By the time she got home, I was asleep. Thursdays were good. I had just had enough the night before to have a little fun and not be hungover. I felt pretty good. Thursdays meant Friday was coming. That night, I would stop for a couple and zip home in time for dinner. Oddly enough, I always seemed to find a six-pack of Bud hiding behind the hot tub on Thursday nights. My life was beginning to resemble the Snoopy cartoon that showed the dog lying flat on Monday and gradually getting upright throughout the week. On Friday, he was dancing. I guess the rest of the story is self-explanatory. The weekend would be a lot of partying. I was one of those closet types. I mean, people knew or suspected, but for a long time they were a little unsure. I was always busy mowing the lawn, changing oil in the cars, working on a project in the shop, and so on. Keeping myself busy was a great way to hide the drinking.

The excuses are some of the best parts. After being a beer drinker for a long time, I could write a book about it. Oh, that's right—I did. You are reading it. Alcoholism does that to you after a while. You forget the little things in life, like where you just were an hour ago. Sometimes you even forget your wife's first name. I had drunk a couple of beers that night. I was introducing her to someone at a party, and I said, "Hi, Jim, this is…this is…uh…my wife."

I remember the look on her face as she piped in, "Lydia! My name is Lydia." We all had a great laugh about that (fourteen years later when she finally forgave me).

I was always trying so hard to hide everything. It is really difficult if you are a closet alcoholic. We hide it very well until we start
to lose control. Once, Lydia complained about all the empty beer
cans in the garage. As far as I know, she could have just been making
a comment. However, we alcoholics are very sensitive people. After
that, I began not only hiding the full ones, but I also started devis-
ing ways to hide the empties. Beer is really hard as it takes so damn
many to get drunk. By the end of the week, I would have a truckload
of empties. So I started smashing the cans up. Unfortunately, the
bottle-and-can-return machines only take the full-size can, not the
squished-up ones. I didn't get my money back for the empties—too
bad for me.

Then there was the wine experiment. Beer gives you this huge
pot gut, so I decided to fool everybody. I would stay skinny and
drink wine. That way, they would never know. The only trouble was
that the wine made me drunker faster. I remember rocking back and
forth in this old, orange chair in the family room. My grandfather
had given it to me. God, how my wife hated that ugly chair. It was
a Biltwell brand and a family heirloom. I was not going to get rid of
it—at least, for a long time.

I would hide my wine bottles in the shop. We would be sitting there watching TV, and I would get up each time during the
advertisements to go to the shop and "check on something I was
gluing together," "check the furnace motor," "make sure the hot-tub
pump was okay," or some lame excuse like that. For a long time, my
wife bought it. Or so I thought. I would do fine for a while. Soon,
however, I would have to start making some other kind of excuse. I
had to pee every five minutes too—that added to the problem. She
would sit there reading a magazine, sewing, or doing something else
while we were watching an old movie or comedy show. Occasionally,
I would hear her mutter something like, "You sure go to the bathroom a lot." The worse it got, the harder it was for me to get out of
that damn orange rocking chair. I would look carefully to my left to
see if she was watching and try to stand up awkwardly without her
noticing. Finally, there was no other way to do it. I had to rock back
and forth real hard and then push upward with my arms, using all

the strength I had. Sometimes I would come up so fast, I would fly forward and almost slam into the door into the garage. I would aim for the brass doorknob and swing the door open so fast, I nearly hit myself in the head with it. I am sure I did a few times as my posture has always been bent slightly forward. Finally, I started leaving the door open so I could zip through it unnoticed. Yeah right. The trouble was that there were two doors to the garage from the family room. The first one led down to a concrete staircase to the basement. The second door went to the garage. There were fourteen hard stairs to the basement. Once in a while I would come flying through there and end up at the bottom of the stairs, full of bruises. Although the basement was carpeted, the bounce down was tough. So I decided to figure out a way to avoid this problem. The plan was always the same—check the view, rock hard three times, lunge forward, step through the first door, grab the second one, open it, and swing into the garage, and I had it made. Next, all I had to do was find the wine bottles, gulp down about six ounces, and slip back into the house, right? Then I had to get through the doors on the way back and land in the chair. Sometimes I would fall into it so hard that the top of the chair would slam into the wall. I kept some Sheetrock repair and paint just out in the garage for those crash landings.

"Are you okay?"

"Yeah, fine. I just missed the last step." *Sure, Ron.*

Whimpering quietly and limping badly, I would slip out the basement door, through a little wooded area, and up to the back door of the shop, where I could grab another drink, and then slip in through the garage, stumbling and thinking I was unnoticed. I will never forget the time I did that and had forgotten to unlock the back of the shop door. Rain was pouring down. I had to turn around and walk back down through the muddy backyard and up the basement stairs again. Lydia started chanting, "Why are you so wet and muddy? Where did you go?"

Oh, shut up, I thought to myself. Knowing she had me, there was no mercy.

"Your shoes are all covered with mud. How did you get so damn dirty? Now there is mud all the way up the stairs and across the family room."

Was this some kind of punishment for my drinking? Probably.

My wife and I always loved little, white dogs. Over the years we had several of them. As long as they were white, weighed less than five pounds, and cost enough to buy a small car, we were happy. I will never forget another time when Mighty, as we called him, was lying quietly right in my path. Thank the stars, my wife was in the bathroom. So there went Mr. Cool flying across the room. I tripped on the dog and landed on my face on the floor. As I fell, all I heard was this awful noise that sounded like a goose getting run over by a dump truck. Down I went, right on top of the dog. Poor little Mighty was limping down the hall and yelping. Out of the bathroom, at a hundred miles an hour, came my wife with her pants halfway down. I tried to pretend I was doing push-ups and everything was fine. I told her I must have somehow scared the dog. Lydia did not buy it. I went to bed early while she held her little dust mop in her lap, scowling at me once again. The dog was okay, but he didn't come near me for a week.

Then there was the time she complained about all the wine bottles filling up the garbage can. *Oops! Caught again.* From that day on, I started this huge process of smashing the wine bottles up into small green pieces (cheap wines were sold in green bottles). Then I would line the bottom of the garbage can with newspaper, pour in the glass, layer it again with more paper, and then stack regular garbage on top of that. I smelled like garbage a lot because throughout the week, I would have to empty out the garbage, lift up the first layer of newspaper, dump more green glass chips in there, and cover it all back up again.

One day I came home from work, and she had arrived earlier than me that day. She was at the end of the driveway, staring at all this broken green glass. There was a big pile of it lying at the edge of the driveway, where the garbage truck picked it up on Monday mornings. Recently, the garbage company had bought these new trucks that had a lift. An arm would come down, close on the can, and lift it up to dump it. The old-fashioned garbageman was gone. Now they just sat in trucks and pulled levers. The arm would grab the can, lift it up, turn it upside down, and shake it violently, removing all the garbage, and then slam it down on the sidewalk. Since then, these machines have improved. Somehow, during all the grabbing, shaking, dumping, and slamming, my great plan had failed. Broken wine-bottle glass now lay everywhere. *Am I still fooling her? Has she figured it out yet? Of course not. She couldn't possibly know I drank too much.* Or so I thought.

Then there were the hard-liquor experiments. I had drunk hard liquor no more than half a dozen times in my life. I didn't do well with the hard stuff. The first time I got really drunk on whiskey, I tried driving an old car about as fast as it would go on a main highway very near a major Portland, Oregon, hospital. At least I had enough sense to do it close to a hospital in case I got injured in a wreck. I guess I really should have done that near a morgue. Another time I drank a lot of rum and ended up in a gay bar somewhere in Portland. I remember trying to dance with a hairy girl. I didn't remember going there, and worse, I didn't remember leaving or how I got home. I think I had a good time though. When I woke up the next morning, my car had some strange marks on it. I hid the car for about a week. When the police didn't show up, I figured it was okay to drive it again. About a month later, one of my drinking buddies told me he was with me on that bender. He told me that my car was all scratched up because I drove into a ditch lined with blackberries. Somehow, we dug our way out of the ditch and managed to get home. The very last time I tried drinking hard liquor, I got my pickup truck stuck between a parking meter and the side of a building. It cost me one hundred and fifty bucks to get it out of that mess. Today it would cost a lot closer to five hundred bucks. I decided that maybe the liquor experiment wasn't such a good idea after all. I would go back to beer.

Toward the end of my drinking, I was working in a prison as an electrician. I didn't find out until later that the inmates used to place bets on how long I would be in the bathroom on Monday mornings. I would somehow get to work, usually with only one eye open and my pounding head resting on the doorframe while driving with one hand. Driving that way with the window open in the middle of the winter in the pouring-down rain was not a whole lot of fun. When I arrived in the prison parking lot, my skin was pulled back so far off my skull that I looked like ET. My hair was pulled back and soaking wet. My clothes were damp, clear to the waist. Somehow, I stumbled in the front door of the joint and made it to the bathroom. Early in the morning, the inmates were all lined up in the maintenance shop, waiting for us to take them out on work assignments. They all wanted to work for Ron on Mondays. They knew it would be an easy day as we would spend most of it sleeping. I would walk in the shop door, wave at my coworkers, and slide into the bathroom. I would be in there for at least an hour. No one bothered me. *Am I still fooling everyone?* I would force caffeine down my throat, throw up, sleep, and suffer from diarrhea. *Isn't drinking fun?* This would go on and off until lunchtime, when I would slip out to my car and go to sleep for an hour or so. Then in the afternoons I would work really hard and fast, trying to make up for the mornings. Those poor inmates I was supervising—I hope none of them ever finds me when they get out of prison. I was so scared of that, I carried a gun for two years after retirement.

As far as the inmates were concerned, here were guys who had done everything from murder to bank robbery, rape, and God only knew what else. They were all laughing at this alcoholic who thought no one knew he drank. The inmates would have something like a football pool. It was called, How Long Will Ron Be in the Bathroom? Side bets were placed on things like what kind of excuses he would have for his "brown bottle" flu.

After I quit drinking, a lot of the inmates were sad. The old prison just wasn't the same, with Ron coming in all bright-eyed and bushy-tailed on Monday mornings. I used to go to prison and tell drinking stories. Now I go to AA and tell prison stories. Ain't life grand? Now I would come in fully rested and ready to do a hard day's work. The other staff and inmates did not know what to do. I was getting so much done around the place, I was making the other employees mad. Then I got called into the office. I knew my number was up. Actually, they promoted me and sent me to a large prison in Salem. I think they were glad to get rid of me. Now, instead of drinking, I poke fun at my past. Why not! Looking back, it is pretty funny that I thought I had everyone fooled. Like my mom always said, "Laugh at the world, and people laugh back at you. Laugh at yourself, and they laugh with you."

Well, what does one do about all this drinking? That is another story.

Are You an Alcoholic?

So I was sitting in this seminar in Vancouver, Washington, at a place called St. Joseph's Hospital in the early 1980s. The company I worked for sent all the managers to numerous education classes each year. The topic that day was on how to deal with alcoholic employees. It was an extremely interesting seminar. After lunch and a couple of beers, I settled in for the afternoon portion of the event. At about 2:00 p.m. the presenter looked across a field of faces and zeroed in on me.

"Sir, are you an alcoholic?"

It was a good thing the auditorium had a high ceiling, because I would have stuffed my head into anything lower. I mean, I came off that chair like a rocket ship. I was furious. Meanwhile, all my coworkers, bosses, and other employees from my company were howling with laughter. There must have been a hundred or more people in that room. I remember saying something like, "How dare you call me an alcoholic in front of all these people?"

The presenter informed me that I asked a lot of questions and had said my family was riddled with alcoholics. Even though she was correct, I was still devastated. Somehow, I had to regain my respect though it was no use. I was trashed. The laughing continued. Then I was offered a way out. The facilitator said to me that if I could quit drinking for a year, then I might not be an alcoholic. That was all I needed—a way out. But after I opened my mouth in an attempt to save face, the laughter reached a new height.

"A year? Is that all? How about ten years? How about that? I will quit drinking for ten years."

The last thing I heard as I stormed out of the building was almost drowned out by the laughter. While I was on my way out, she left me with a parting shot.

"Good luck with that one, sir. I doubt you make it a week."

Now most drinkers would have a real problem with something like this. But I am a stubborn Irish German. I remember thinking that I would show those naysayers I could do it. The following Monday morning, they were all lined up around my desk at work. I was feeling like crap, but I had made it through the first leg—three days. When I got to a year without a drink, people at work started to take notice. I wanted to win this bet so badly that I even went to some twelve-step meetings. I didn't tell anyone from work or even my wife. The first call to that lady was like notifying someone that I had won a lottery.

"Hi there. This in Ron Weber. I met you about a year ago when—"

"Yeah, I remember you. So how'd it go? You didn't make it, did you?"

"Yes, I did! I made it an entire year without a drink. I am *not* an alcoholic."

"You said ten years. Remember that? Try it again, and call me in a year."

Then the phone went dead. My blood started to boil. *How dare she?* Then I decided that a deal was a deal. Every year for ten years I called that woman up and said that I had made it again. Before I could utter another sound, she would always say the same thing and hang up.

"Try it again."

Although I hated her, I was not going to give in. At the end of my alleged contract, I informed her that I had done all ten years as I said I would, and just to prove that I was not an alcoholic, I would do one more year. She said to me, "Good job. Maybe you are not an alcoholic after all. When you finish another year, why don't you go try some controlled drinking and see how that works out for you?"

A year later the bet was done. I won—eleven years without a cold one. I was off to the bar for a few beers. I couldn't wait. *Glug, glug, glug.* But a short time later I was sitting in an AA meeting, accepting a newcomer's chip—so much for the beer experiment. I suppose I should have known. I mean, normal drinkers don't ask the kind of questions I did at the seminar over a decade earlier. They also don't go around making a big deal about how much their parents drank and how I wasn't going to turn out like them. Normal drinkers surely don't make stupid bets like I did. I mean, really? Refuse to drink for over a decade just to prove to others that you are not an alcoholic? That was dumb, really dumb. After eleven years without a drink, followed by a short attempt at drinking beer normally, I gave up. My last drink was in September of 1995.

CHAPTER 4

THE JUVENILE DELINQUENT

My delinquent behavior started at about the age of ten years old. I was mowing a lawn for Mrs. Randall up the street. It was a tiny, flat yard. When it was time to pay, she only gave me about twenty-five cents. I was so mad that the following week when I mowed her lawn again, I decided to get back at her. When she went to get her purse, I saw a small jar full of change, sitting on a bookshelf by the front door. I grabbed the jar, tipped it up, and got about three bucks in change. When she came back, I accepted another quarter from her, thanked her, and went on my way. Over sixty years later I still know God is going to get me for that. I hope he doesn't spank people. My dad did too much of that, and I don't want any more of it.

Then at the age of twelve my friend Gary and I went into a store and stole a bag of marbles. We walked to the Vista Bridge in Portland. Today it is still called the Suicide Bridge because so many people have jumped off it, landing exactly one hundred and twenty feet down onto Canyon Road. Fortunately, fences have been put all along both sides of the bridge, making the jump much harder to do.

At the top of the bridge we patiently waited for something big coming up Canyon Road. After about fifteen minutes we saw it. A Greyhound bus carrying about thirty passengers on their way to the city of Seaside at the Oregon Coast was stopped at a red light around seven blocks away. We tore open the stolen bag of marbles and divided them in half. Just before the bus got to the bridge, we dropped our load like two bomber pilots from WWII. About three seconds later our payload hit the target one hundred and twenty feet below. About a hundred glass marbles of numerous pretty colors hit the top of that bus like ten machine guns. The bus came to a complete stop, and the driver stepped out. At first, he might have thought it was hail, but when he looked up and saw two little juvenile delinquents laughing our heads off, he knew better. Gary and I must have run about three miles and hid under our beds. He lived up a long hill to the Council Crest area, and I went west up Canyon Road to my home. We didn't talk to each other for a month.

While I don't remember which one of us spilled the beans, it was something I will never forget. Gary's parents had come over for dinner with him. My dad was in the insurance business and was always inviting people over or going out to restaurants to talk business with them. We were sitting in the dining room, eating dinner, and one of us (sorry, Gary, I think it was you) whispered something about the incident, and my dad overheard us.

I guess you don't have to wonder what happened. I got the belt. Gary got the same when he went home. Three days later we went down to the store where the one-dollar theft took place and apologized to the manager. Dad took the cost of the marbles out of my allowance, and I got the belt again when we got home. Was it worth it? Hell, yes. Back in those days, kids did stuff like that. Today it is different. Life is just a lot more complicated.

When I was a kid, the City of Portland built the Oregon Zoo walking distance from our house. It is a sixty-four-acre massive complex. They also put up the Oregon Museum of Science and Industry (OMSI) across the parking lot and a small golf course up the hill. For two years we would ride our bicycles or walk over there and drive all the contractors crazy. The construction was so massive that it was just open to anyone. We would walk in all the cages we could get into. Where the lions, tigers, and bears would soon live, we played. We would swing in the monkey cages and run in the fields where the giraffes would. We rode our bicycles where the elephants would live. Some of the contractors would get mad and chase us away. Some paid no attention to us. As the zoo neared completion, we were kicked out for good.

Across the parking lot was OMSI. As they were building that, we did the same thing. It was smaller and under more control. One night after they kicked us out, we were able to break in at night. As the structure wasn't completely finished, it was also not fully secure. My brother Bob and I snuck in, and he took an oscilloscope, which was basically a TV tube for those big, old televisions. Bob somehow made a lamp out of it, which we kept in his bedroom for years. I stole something too; however, I cannot remember what it was.

At the twelve-hole small golf course, six holes were up a hill and out of sight of the clubhouse. As my grandfather owned a big golf course on the Oregon Coast, we had access to golf clubs. We would take some clubs to our home in Portland and go to that small course near the zoo. As we didn't have any money, we would just play the back six holes as they were called. But we always had to keep an eye out for the owners and employees. Not too long after we started playing up there, they noticed us. When they went back to the clubhouse and found out we hadn't paid, they would come after us. As we had a huge uphill advantage, they could never catch us. When they got more aggressive in their efforts to catch us, we stopped playing there. I was really mad about that, so I designed a revenge plan.

I had this dog named Blacky, who followed me everywhere except school. He actually did that once, and I had to leave him outside all day in the rain. The Catholic nuns wouldn't let him in, and I fully understood. He was a bit like me, always looking for trouble. After that day Blacky stayed home. Sitting outside in the rain for six hours once was enough for him. While we did have bus service, I was picked on all the time and just enjoyed the three- or four-mile walk by myself. I did that for many years unless the weather was really bad. Then I just had to put up with the bullies.

One day I was walking near the zoo complex, and I went past the golf course. I was on a dead-end road with Blacky right by my side. He loved to pick fights with other dogs, so I had to keep him close. I suddenly heard a loud voice yelling, "Fore." He was just being courteous as the course was small, and there was not a lot of room out there between holes. It was at the tenth hole on the course, and the green was about forty feet from the dead-end road. There were also several holes in an old fence that separated the neighborhood and the course. Blacky heard the *plop* the ball made when it hit the center of the green, only about two or three feet from the hole. It was a great shot, but Blacky had better ideas, at least for him. He got through the fence and went straight for the ball. He immediately fetched the ball and brought it to me. He dropped it at my feet, barking happily and with tail wagging. I could see this "do it again" look in his eyes.

Meanwhile the golfer was furious. He came running down the hill, yelling loudly. I waited at the fence, apologized, and told him to place the ball about two feet from the hole. I then complimented him for his great shot. He seemed pleased with that, he took the ball, and I left. About a block away, I was patting Blacky all over. *Good boy.* When we got home, I tossed the rubber balls and started playing fetch with Blacky, using golf balls. For the next three or four months, I would go over to that same dead-end street with Blacky all the way. He could feel the excitement. We would hide behind some bushes, and when he heard the *plop*, off he went. We would do that a couple of times and then take off. Then we would walk uphill to the back six holes, and Blacky would grab anything as long as it was white, small, and hard. He had golf ball fever. And so did I as I started flipping the golfers off with the middle finger while my dog was running away with their ball. After several angry golfers went furiously to the clubhouse about the shitty little kid with red hair and his bastard ball-stealing black dog, the staff would jump on their riding lawn mowers and chase after me. But I was long gone by then. I went up there about once a week for a whole summer. I thought about writing them a letter and telling them, "Either let me play on the back six holes for free, or I will keep sending my ball-stealing mutt out there." Then one day sometime after that, I met a girl and gave up the golf-ball game. Girls were better. Blacky never forgave me.

Freckles Runs Away (Again)

One of the first girls I went after was a total disaster. I was walking around in Downtown Portland, and I saw this cute girl. She was sitting on a bench and smiled at me. I just stood there talking to her and noticed she was shaking. It was about thirty degrees outside, and she did not even have a jacket on. When I asked her about it, she said she didn't have one. So I got her one. I went into a store, took off my jacket, put on a girl's coat, and then put my jacket over the top of it and walked out without paying. Fortunately, no clerk saw me. She thought that was cute. We went and had lunch as she was hungry and didn't have any money. In the course of our meal she told me that she had run away from a small town near the Canadian border. She started crying and wanted to go home. But she was broke. I walked her to the Greyhound Bus Depot and bought two tickets. I still had a few bucks from winning some games in a pool hall that week. A few hours later, we were on our way.

We left about 11:00 p.m. and would arrive early next morning. We just hung out until it was time to get on the bus. We really hit it off great. We laughed and talked. Finally, she fell asleep on my shoulder, and I was in love. When we arrived, I thought we would rent a room, get some jobs, get married, and have a great life. Instead, she called her mom. A half hour later her mom and dad showed up. He told me to leave his little girl alone or he would kill me. She got in the car and left. There I was, fourteen years old, divorced, and brokenhearted. I took the next bus back to Portland. When I got home, I was grounded for two weeks.

Chopping Down a Building

Most people with axes chopped down trees. But I had a better idea. About five blocks from our house, half a mile west of the zoo, there was a huge equestrian center. Next to it was a large brickmaking company. When I was around thirteen years old, the land was deemed too valuable for what was there currently. The brick company was a filthy and noisy business that belonged miles away in some industrial complex, not one block from a neighborhood of nice homes. Likewise, the equestrian center was not doing well. People were a lot more interested in cars than in horses. The stink from both the brick company and the equestrian center horse manure infuriated the neighborhood. On the other side, the Oregon Zoo was finished, the OMSI was up and running, and the golf course was doing well. Investors were looking for land to build more housing and office buildings. Pressure was on for the existing business to shut down. Eventually, the brick company moved, and finally, the equestrian center closed its doors.

While the brick company moved everything out and demolished their buildings, investors took a closer look at the equestrian center. Instead of demolishing it, they gutted the huge building and left the exterior beams. They thought maybe they could use the roof and outer beams and build inward from there. But the wood, ceilings, and high roof stank from decades of horses and the manure that went with them. Investors argued, and finally, one of them purchased the property and decided to develop it himself.

For about three months the sole investor thought about either keeping the outer structure or just knocking it down. He would be able to have the structure dismantled and sell what he could. Then he would build new office buildings. One day I was playing out there with Blacky. I would take him to that property and let him run around and around. I would throw balls, chase him, and just play around with my best friend, my big, black dog. I used to climb up those beams and anywhere else I could get to. The structure was like a giant fort. One day a nosy neighbor was outside when I was walking home. She told me that they were going to tear the place down soon, and I shouldn't be playing there as it was not safe. That old building might fall down on me. But I would pay no attention to the old bag. I kept right on playing there.

Slowly, over the next few summer days, I noticed equipment starting to show up. The old gal was right. The building was coming down. My big fort would disappear. I became outraged and decided to tear it all down myself. Every day I went there early in the morning with an ax. I chopped and chopped for days. Every whack with the ax was hitting my dad back for all the times he hit me. The building was approximately the size of a square city block in length and half that distance wide. You are talking about two hundred feet by one hundred feet. There was about a dozen gigantic beams around two feet thick and twenty-five or more feet tall. My plan looked impossible and dangerous. I didn't care. If these bastards were going to take my fort, I would be the one to knock it down. However, the owner had other ideas.

One day I noticed two men in suits and ties off in the distance, staring at me. They looked at me for a long time as I chopped away. I would chop for an hour on one beam and then move on to the next one. I slowly worked my way around the superthick beams one at a time. I wanted the whole thing to come down evenly. As I continued that day, the men began to move forward in my direction. I told Blacky, "Kill!" He went tearing after them, and they ran back to their car, quickly driving away. Two days later I noticed a lone man in overalls, watching me. I called Blacky, but noticed the man had a big German shepherd on a lease with him. He walked slowly toward me while I hung on to Blacky.

"What are you doing there, young fellow?"

"They are taking away my fort, so I am chopping it down myself."

"Do you know who owns this structure?"

"No."

"I do."

The man spoke calmly and seemed like a nice guy. He went on to explain that some professionals were coming the following week, and we should let them do the job safely. He explained that a structure that size could shift with the slightest wind if I had kept on chopping. The building would collapse in an instant, and my dog and I would be crushed to death before we could get clear.

I just stood there embarrassed. The man said that the beams I chopped away on were damaged although they could be salvaged by cutting them about two feet shorter. They would still be sellable, just for less money.

"Do you have any money to pay me for what you did?

"No."

I apologized the best I could. I was told that the two men watching me a couple of days before were private detectives he had hired to find out who was damaging the beams. They had followed me from a distance that day and knew where I lived. While I thought I was going to a juvenile jail for this, the guy seemed calm about the whole affair.

"Is your dad at home? We should go talk to him."

"I don't have a dad. He beat the hell out of us kids and slapped my mom around. The police threw him out, and my mom has a restraining order on him. He lives in a cabin deep in the woods on Mount Hood. I haven't seen him in years."

By this time, I was crying. The man thought for a minute and asked me if I would be willing to work off the damage at his own house. He needed help with his yard work. I didn't think about it for a single second. I just said yes. I believe he just felt sorry for me. The following day he picked me up and drove into a neighborhood of some of the most expensive homes in Portland. It was just across the highway and up in the woods from where the building that I had damaged was. His home was one of the biggest houses I had ever seen. An electric gate segregated his palace from the outside world. Along one side of the long driveway, I noticed small train tracks. When we got to the house, a small train sat off to one side of the house. I would learn that the train actually worked and could accommodate about six people and went all over the several-acre compound. The house had about eight bedrooms and looked like something out of a James Bond movie. To the right of the house sat a six-bay garage with numerous antique or luxury automobiles. This guy was superrich. But oddly, he never acted like it. He never got mad at me or even raised his voice. He just treated me like I was part of the family. He told me what to do, and I did it. There was a lot of hedge trimming, mowing, and weeding.

Often throughout the summer I was allowed to use the train to carry dirt, rocks, fertilizers, and anything else needed for the acres of bushes, shrubs, trees, gravel paths, and more. It was really fun to drive. I worked from the middle of June to the middle of August about three days a week. Over the two months I really began to realize how odd my family was. This man had a lovely wife and several adorable kids. They interacted like a normal family should. There was no hitting, no yelling, and no belittling. I wanted to move in.

At the end of the summer we agreed that I had made proper restitution for my behavior. The man surprised me by giving me some money. In the end, I had been exposed to how a real family should function. I lost a fort, but had found a train.

One of the things that started my juvenile-delinquency behavior was not having a dad around. He left when I was ten, and it was kind of a license to hang out with other kids like me and get into trouble. My mother was busy working and raising four kids. She did the best she could, but it was difficult for her to keep track of all of us, especially when I would sneak out at night. I would put a tall ladder out the front of my window and go see what kind of mischief I could get into. When asked why there was a ladder out by my window, I lied and told her I was going to clean my windows. I knew she didn't buy that, so I had to change things up. I put the ladder away. That was on a Sunday. The following weekend, I waited until my mom was asleep. I unlocked my window and quietly tiptoed down to the basement and left the house. It was very important to take other steps. I would put three pillows under the bed blankets to make it look like someone was in the bed. This was important as my bedroom was right across from the bathroom on the main floor, and Mom's room was right next to mine. She got up often in the middle of the night to pee and would crack my door a bit to see if anyone was in the bed. And because she suspected I was going out at night, she would check the locks. There was a side door down a hall, a front door across the house, and two doors out of the basement. Sometimes on weekends she would check all four door locks when she got up once in the middle of the night. So when I left, I would make sure that I would lock the door on my way out.

Where I went depended on who was able and willing. One friend was named Jeff. We would walk all over the neighborhood, just talking and laughing. Sometimes we would turn over garbage cans or rub a cube of butter on someone's window. It was mostly just childish misbehavior. Jeff's parents had an old French car. I think it might have been a Peugeot or something like that. It was a tiny car that might have even had only three wheels. We would push it up the driveway from the carport. Then we would coast it down a long hill and start it up. We would drive all over the place, and then on the way home, we would turn the motor off about a block up the road and coast it back into the carport. We did these many times over a couple of years. We were about fifteen years old at that time. On one occasion I walked up to his house at midnight on a Saturday. We had no phones except those noisy old, black dial phones, and only adults were allowed to touch them. We would have to make plans a day or two earlier. On this particular week, I did not see him playing on the streets after school, and as he did not go to my Catholic school, I had not seen him for a few days. I just decided to go knock on his basement bedroom window. As I approached his house that night, I saw the Peugeot. The whole front end and one side were smashed to pieces. I walked past the house without stopping. A couple of days later another friend in the neighborhood told me that Jeff took the car out on the Friday night before and crashed it. As he was a year younger than me and did not have the driving skills I did, I always told him to never go out alone. Sadly, he did on Friday night and lost control. His parents found out that I had been teaching him how to drive, and I was never allowed in that house again.

When I could not find someone in the neighborhood, I would walk three miles to my best friend's house. Mostly, we just walked around in the middle of the night. Then we met a real troublemaker walking around about midnight one time. His name was Fritz, and he liked breaking windows on cars with rocks. He just turned out to be too much trouble, and I quit hanging around him. The last I heard he was breaking into houses and stealing things. He went to jail.

Another thing I used to like to do was walk two miles into Portland. It was here that I first found Wayne's Billiards Academy. The place was a pool hall and a hangout for a lot of troublemakers. I also loved walking around in Downtown Portland. I mean, there I was, fourteen years old and running around with a pack of juvenile delinquents in a big city. One of our favorite tricks was making a lot of noise. When the cops would come, we would all run in different directions. With their uniforms, a baton, a gun, and those heavy boots on, they were not fast enough to catch us. And they did not have portable radios, so once they left their car, they had no ability to call for help.

On one occasion, my mom caught me sneaking out. I always left my bedroom window unlocked as when I came back home, all the doors would be locked. I would drag the big ladder from the left side of our house over to the back, where my bedroom was. I would climb up the ladder and crawl into my room. Then I would creep quietly down the stairs into the basement, go out the back door, replace the ladder where it was stored, go back into the basement, lock the door, and then quietly sneak upstairs to my bedroom. On one particular night, when I climbed into the bed, I felt something different. It was my mother's unshaven legs. She got fed up with me sneaking out and her not being able to catch me red-handed. She pulled the covers back and got into my bed and fell asleep. When I climbed into bed that night, I woke her up—*busted*. I was grounded for a solid month. Even that didn't stop me. I think my mom finally gave up, because I never got caught again.,

When I was about fifteen, I started taking my mom's car on Saturday nights. She often would have a couple of drinks on week-end nights, so she slept like a log, and I was running loose. One particular night, when I was fourteen or fifteen, I went to Downtown Portland to the pool hall and got some friends. When they heard I had a car, they were on their feet, running down the stairs. We would drive all over town and get into whatever mischief we could.

Tacoma Whitey

I was never much of a pool player. I tried my best, but I would never be much more than adequate. As far as money games were, I won some and lost some. Going to Wayne's Billiards Academy was a great thrill though. Most places like this were dives or in a corner bar with one dim light over the table and sloppy drunks trying to hit the ball. Pool halls always had a bad reputation. When Wayne put his place together, it was first-class. There must have been about twenty or more tables. The place was on a second floor above a celebrated restaurant that had been there for decades. One whole wall was solid glass about fifty feet long. There were fancy bright lights all over the big room. Wayne's place was truly a billiards academy instead of an old pool hall. For years I would watch the pros battle it out.

One of the highlights of Wayne's was professional players. They came from all over the country on tours. When someone big was coming, you had to get there early so you could see the game. The place would be packed with onlookers, and the big room would have cigarette smoke from the floor to the ceiling. No alcohol was allowed, but some snuck in whiskey flasks. There would be a lot of cheering, moaning, and sometimes even booing. We had our local favorites, and we didn't like outsiders coming in and walking away with local money. The games themselves would be for money—sometimes lots of money. And the side betting was there too. I was much better at gambling on the players than playing pool myself, so I mostly did that. The professionals took their wins and losses like gentlemen. Most of them were decked out in suede shoes, fancy suits, and expensive hats. Diamond rings on their fingers and gold watches on their wrists were standard as were diamond-studded pool cues with gold rings around the shaft. It was quite a circus. However, the nonprofessional players like me were not gentlemen most of the time. When some of us lost our bets on games, foul language and fistfights were on the menu. Those who won cheered and laughed. Often the winners had to duck out the door quickly before someone beat the crap out of them and took their money back out of spite. Often, they were just poor sports who would complain that the table wasn't level, or the felt on the table was flawed. Although people loved to win, they really hated to lose.

One Saturday morning, when Wayne's had just opened up, some big guys in fancy suits came through the door. They were just standing at the top of the stairs, looking around. I was cleaning tables and emptying the ashtrays for free table time. The vacuuming belonged to a regular janitor. His name was Rubin Wolf. Wayne helped him by making sure he always had a few bucks in his pocket. Rubin was the oddest person I had ever known at that time. He was mentally challenged though he could handle simple conversations. He could also be a nice guy. However, he had two very odd habits. The first was that when he turned on a vacuum cleaner, he would start yelling and running. He would be looking back like someone was chasing him. Wayne told me when Rubin turned on the vacuum cleaner, ghosts would start chasing him. The look on his face was terrifying as he zoomed up and down the isles between the pool tables. When he was finished, he would let out a huge sigh of relief and put the vacuum away, until the next time. The other odd habit was something he sang—one little jingle—over and over, all day long. He would be walking around, helping me brush the tables, and doing other chores while singing.

"Rubin Grady...dee da dee."

It was just something that was stuck in his head. I never knew who Rubin Grady was, and I am not sure Rubin did either. Maybe Grady was his middle name. But it always made him happy, so we were happy for him. Sixty years later I can still hear him singing that. Now I do it myself sometimes. Suddenly, a deep and loud voice rang out across the whole room.

"Where's Whitey?"

The room fell silent.

"Rubin Gra—"

Rubin's little chime was interrupted as the voice rang out again.

"Where the fuck is Tacoma Whitey?"

At that moment Rubin dropped what he was doing and ran for the utility room, where the mops and buckets were stored. His face was white, and his hands were shaking. He closed himself inside. His whimpering voice could be heard through the door.

Wayne looked scared and was just standing there, frozen in place. These guys were real thugs, and now they were staring at Wayne to the point where he had to answer them.

"He's in the bathroom."

At that precise moment a disheveled little man came out of the bathroom. He couldn't have been any taller than five feet eight inches and weighed around a hundred and forty pounds. His clothes were wrinkled, his hair scrambled, and he looked like he hadn't shaved in three days or more. His eyes were bloodshot, and he looked really sick.

The thugs came to play pool. Whitey had beaten one of them really bad in Seattle the week before for hundreds of dollars, and he agreed to give the guy a chance to get his money back with a rematch in Portland on that Saturday morning. There was a gentlemen's agreement in place with pool players. The loser got a second chance. While the big guy from LA was ready to play, the great Tacoma Whitey wasn't. He was an alcoholic and had been on a three-day run. His hands were shaking, and he was sick to his stomach. Wayne got him some coffee, and I went down to the restaurant below and got him something to eat. Tacoma Whitey was one of the best players in the West Coast. He was sort of a "Dapper Dan" kind of guy. Today he looked like a poodle that had been in a fight with a rottweiler. In fact, he probably had gotten into a bar fight while on his binge. The rottweiler in this case was the guy from LA. I have forgotten his name all these years later although he too was a top contender in the West Coast. Today was the rematch.

After some coffee and food, Wayne pulled out an electric razor from under the front desk. In a few minutes Whitey looked a bit more like himself. The match was to start at 10:00 a.m. Whitey had blown every penny. Wayne never loaned anyone money for competitions. It was just a bad bet, and he never did it. Rubin, who had come out of the closet and was sitting quietly in a corner, did not have any money. His "dee da dee" was silent. As this was a private competition, no one knew about it. I was the only other person in the room. Whitey, who didn't know me from Adam or Eve, walked over to me and asked me to loan him some money. The deal was that if he won, I would get half the winnings. I liked that idea. Unfortunately, I had spent most of my lawn-mowing money the past week. The night before, I had won ten dollars in a small-time match, and that was all I had. Whitey was in a panic. So he decided to go with the truth. He told the goons that all he had was ten bucks because he had blown all his money, drinking. The three men started howling with laughter. Then the other player blew up.

"You little fuck. You drag me down from Seattle for ten damn bucks. Well, fine, you little prick. I'm gonna take your ten bucks, and then I'm gonna give it back to the little freckle-faced kid. I can't believe you would take money from a poor kid who mowed lawns for it. Shame on you!"

One basic rule on rematches was a time limit. They had two hours to battle it out. When 10:00 a.m. arrived, the two men shook hands. The match was on. A few minutes later, the first game was over. Whitey had won. Now we had twenty bucks. The guys from LA were laughing and taunting Whitey for being a disheveled drunk and taking money from a kid. However, at the end of one hour, Whitey was up five hundred dollars. The guys from LA were no longer laughing. While the game went up and down from there, Whitey was still well on a big win. When the two-hour timer rang, Tacoma Whitey had done the impossible. Out of a three-day drunk, he had proven his skills. He walked out of there with a thousand bucks. The guy from LA did the gentleman thing. He shook Whitey's hand and complimented his playing. The three men left quietly.

By this time, a lot of regular patrons had shown up to play pool for fun. When they saw a big game going on, they forgot about anything else. They did not know the arrangement Whitey and I had. When he called me over and laid five hundred bucks on the table, the room fell silent.

"A deal is a deal, kid. Here's your money."

The great Tacoma Whitey thanked me and walked out of Wayne's Billiards Academy. I was in heaven. I had never had so much money in my entire life though my trip to heaven was short. I felt like that poodle and was looking at thirty rottweilers. Everyone was trying to borrow money or get me to play pool for money. I got really scared and walked into the bathroom. I could hear them all reveling in jealousy because any of them had more than ten bucks in their pocket and would have gladly backed Whitey in a game. They just weren't there. I was the lucky guy who was at the right place and right time. Being the coward I was, I slipped out of the bathroom and ran down the stairs and out the door.

So what was I going to do with five hundred bucks? I decided I needed to buy one of those supercool pool cues—no more using the crummy ones at Wayne's. The great Ron Weber would become a famous pool player with his expensive cue. Off I went to a billiards equipment company. Fifty dollars later I had a really nice pool cue. And for another ten bucks I got a leather case. In the early 1960s that was a lot of money. My great pool-playing days didn't last very long. When I first walked into Wayne's with that cue, a lot of the guys laughed at me. To own a cue like that, I needed to be a lot better player. I took some lessons and did improve. Two months later I had lost all that money. Finally, I put my fancy pool cue up as collateral, and I lost that too. I was back to where I started—a skinny, freckle-faced, red-haired little kid who mowed lawns. I didn't go back to Wayne's for about a year. But life was still good because I said so.

Runnin' from the Cops

I learned to run early as my father used to get drunk and chase us. If he caught us, it was the dreaded belt. God, he hit hard. I soon learned that if I outran him, it was like a bonus win. I mean, first of all, I didn't get the beating, and secondly, I didn't have to worry about him coming after me the next day, because he would be so hungover, he wouldn't remember being mad at me. By the time I was about five, I could outrun him. Our Catholic grade school didn't have a track team. Too bad, I would have been a star runner.

One day my next-door friend was flaunting his allowance. I got mad and grabbed a dollar from his hand and was running around with it. Steve was crying and wanted it back. Even though it was just some silly nonsense and teasing, my dad heard the ruckus and went ballistic. He ran out on the street while pulling his belt out. He was going to beat the hell out of me. I ran over to Steve and apologized. I gave him the dollar back, and he was fine. We are still friends nearly seventy years later. Unfortunately, my dad was still coming after me.

I was about seven years old and a good runner already. I ran around our 1949 Chrysler and noticed Dad stumbling. He was pretty drunk. I just kept running around the car. Round and round I went. Dad got so dizzy, he fell down.

"Goddamn you. You little shit. If I ever get ahold of you, I'm gonna kill ya."

By this time, he was so sick, he threw up. I took off for the woods. I stayed out there all night in the cold. In the morning he was still passed out on his bed, snoring like an angry lion. After school I came home, and his car was gone. He sold insurance and probably went to the office. Just before dinner, he showed up, and nothing was said. He was a bit drunk already and had forgotten the whole incident of the day before.

Another running exercise was from a highway overpass to the nearby forest. We lived about five blocks from a busy highway. The overpass to the Portland Zoo was another five blocks. My mischievous friends and I would go down there on snowy winter days. We would make snowballs and throw them down onto the busy highway, trying to hit cars. I am not sure what drove me to do that. My mother would say it was my curly, red Irish hair and my gobs of freckles along with a streak of angry Irish.

We would watch all the cars coming and pick one. We were careful not to hit a car with an athletic young man. He might catch us. We also would not hit a car with a woman driver or a car with small children in it. That pretty much left the older men on their way to work. We would pick the car, wave politely to the driver, who most often would smile and wave back as they thought we were just some nice kids having fun. He was right about the fact that we were having fun, but he just did not know what kind of fun (or mischief) we were up to.

Between the time we finished waving and the time the car passed under the overpass was two to three seconds. Wave back to them with the left hand while holding a hard snow- or ice ball behind your back in your right hand, and then throw it straight down onto the car.

Smack!

Now there was a slight problem with all this. This overpass had an on-and-off ramp on both sides. The driver sometimes would hit the brakes after passing under the overpass and getting hit. About five hundred feet ahead he could do a full U-turn and come zooming up the down ramp. It didn't happen often, but when it did, it was a circus show. First, when he hit the brakes, the car started sliding all over the place. Finally, when he got the car under control, he spun all over again while making the U-turn. By now he was really mad and floored it, steaming with anger. He was gonna kill those damn kids. When he finally got on top of the overpass, we were a hundred yards up a steep hill, getting ready to disappear into the forest in front of us. We gave him one final wave, and he gave us back the middle finger. Twenty minutes later, when the coast was clear, we went back and did it again. By noon it was time to get out of our wet clothes and dry out by the fire in our basement. Mom made some grilled cheese sandwiches and hot chocolate. We all sat down by the warm fire and watched Superman on TV. Life was good.

In the off-season of the snowy days, we decided one year to use mud balls and, sometimes, small rocks. This didn't turn out well. It was too dramatic. People could have been really hurt as they were driving a lot faster than they did during the snow season. Also, the police got wind of what we were doing and started patrolling the area too. Although it was easy to outrun them in their uniforms, we were going to get in serious trouble at some point. Although we could easily lose them in the woods, eventually, they would have started knocking on doors, and sooner or later, we would have been arrested. Besides, Superman would not have approved of our behavior. So we ended the mud-balls-and-rocks experiment.

Sometime after that, a little girl was killed about a hundred miles south of Portland when someone threw a rock from an overpass. When it hit, the windshield shattered, and the rock hit her in the head. She died instantly. After the death of that little girl, the Oregon Department of Transportation started putting up mesh fences on overpasses. Today there are fences over many overpasses on highways and freeways. When I saw that article in the *Oregonian* newspaper along with her picture, I got sick to my stomach. Decades later I still think about her. My friends and I stopped throwing things off the bridge at cars. Instead, we started building forts in the woods—smart decision.

I have a lot of remorse for those angry years. Later in life a counselor told me I was angry because my dad was a drunk and he beat me a lot. I was also told that I was mad and ashamed about being the only kid in my Catholic school without a father at home. We were like outcasts. When we went to church on Sundays, hundreds of families were there. Every single family had a father standing next to his wife and children in the church pews—except for my mom. Catholics were not allowed to divorce then, so my mom said she would be dad's lawfully wedded wife until she died. I know it was hard on my mom, standing there alone in those church pews. People whispered and asked her embarrassing questions for years. I was teased about it at school. I felt like I was bad and it was my fault that my dad left. Thus, I had anger issues about it for a long time, and I took it out on others with my delinquent behavior.

I even took it out on my school. One weekend night two of my friends and I were walking around the school, just hanging out. We started talking about how mean the nuns were and how we hated school. We also didn't like how hard-nosed the parish priest was. After a bit I just stood up and threw a rock at a classroom window. It made this awful sound as the glass shattered and hit the floor inside a classroom. Suddenly, we all started laughing. We had stolen some beers from one of the other kids' dad and were drunk. Then we just started throwing more rocks. I don't know how many windows we broke, but it was, at least, several. Then we ran off laughing through the woods back to our houses.

Amends

For a long time, I never thought about it again. Then about twenty years later I was sitting in front of a sponsor in Alcoholics

Anonymous. He was helping me learn how to make amends for my not-so-good behavior in the past. Although causing damage like that was serious and destructive, my amends twenty years later were a bit humorous. There I stood at the receptionist's desk of St. Thomas More Grade School. I was married, owned a business, and was the father of two wonderful sons. I was a soccer coach. My wife was a grade-school teacher. In all aspects, we looked like what every successful family should be. But there I stood, in front of a school employee, about to spill the beans of my former juvenile delinquency.

"Can I help you?"

"Uh, do you have a restroom? Uh, no, that is not exactly why I am here. Uh, you see... A long time ago I got drunk and broke some windows here at the school. Then I kept drinking, and now I go to a twelve-step group and have a sponsor. My sponsor told me I had to make amends for the bad stuff I did in life, and I am sorry for breaking those windows."

With my voice stuttering, I handed her an envelope with two hundred and fifty dollars in it, turned on my heels like a marine drill sergeant, and headed for the door. Then it happened. *Oh god, no. Please don't do this to me.* I had dark glasses on, a mustache, long hair, and a stocking cap. I looked like a guy getting ready to rob a bank. The old gal still recognized me. Maybe it was my voice. She must have been eighty years old. What was she still doing here?

"Wait. Is that you? Aren't you little Ronnie Weber? You're June Weber's little baby boy, aren't you?"

Argh! Holy crap! I turned and took my hat and dark glasses off. There she was, the old church secretary. With my face now the color of a fully ripened Red Delicious Washington State apple, I could only mutter, "Oh, hi, Mrs. B. Uh, nice to see you. Wow, you're still here."

I think she retired right after that as she had probably suspected me from the beginning and was waiting all these years for me to come back and apologize. She could now go home to her great-grandchildren, satisfied that she and the FBI had finally gotten their man. However, the story wasn't over yet. It would only get worse...far worse. Mrs. B was so excited about my honesty and willingness to make amends that she called for the parish priest to come out and meet me. My face was now even redder. I waited for him to come out with a paddle and give me spats like I used to get in school. God, those things would hurt.

Although it seemed like an eternity of waiting, he finally came out. Thank God, he was not the priest who had been there for twenty-plus years when I was growing up. While I was in the Army, he had moved on, and now we had someone else. The new priest was a mean-looking tall guy. I feared he might give me spats because of what I did. Then he would get mad at me because I left and was now going to an Episcopalian church. My mother had moved out of our big home and into a small house one block from the church. When I came back from the military years earlier, I stayed with Mom for three years while going to college. The fact that I only went to the church masses about five times during those years didn't sit well with her. While sitting there waiting for that parish priest, I could hear what I thought he would be saying to me.

For God's sake, Ron, your mother goes to church seven days a week and sings in the choir. You couldn't walk two hundred feet once a week for a one-hour church service?

No, Father, I used to drink a lot and was too hungover to go to mass. Twelve "Our Father's" and twenty "Hail Mary's."

Then he would take my check and give me ten spats for the rock-throwing incident and ten more for not going to church enough. Suddenly, I snapped out of my day dreaming as I saw him entering the room.

Instead of railing on me, the priest just stood there looking at me for about a minute, then walked over and shook my hand. He thanked me for finally coming back to make things right. Then he went back into his office. Why do people always do that? You go to apologize for some really cruddy thing you did, and they thank you for your honesty. Why don't they just smack your hands with a wooden ruler and tell you to get out? I guess it is all part of the forgiveness thing.

Another delinquent incident involving Freckles happened in 1959. It was a when the old priest was still there. I was about twelve years old, and I was a great rock thrower. I could hit almost anything.

Oddly, it gained me some popularity, and it made me feel good. Often it was just hitting a school garbage can, a tree, or anything else. One day we were hanging around after school and watching cars go by on this small road. One of the kids dared me to hit a car. I didn't want to do it, but all the kids started chanting and egging me on. Finally, I said I would, just to get them off my back.

We waited for the right car, and soon it came. The car was an early 1950s four-door sedan. It was a huge car and would be easy to hit. I decided to call a window. As the car approached, I called out, "Right front window!"

I had picked out the best rock I could find. It had to be a certain size and as round as it could be. I had it in my hand, and it felt perfectly warm. I would have to throw it about three hundred feet. I made my mental calculations for the moving car. I was ready. I took a deep breath, wound up like a pitcher for the New York Yankees, and made the throw.

Smack!

The sound could be heard for blocks. The crowd roared. I was a hero…although not for long. We ran up in the woods in all directions and hid. After about twenty minutes, I thought I could run home without being caught. Just as I was about to leave, I heard all this ruckus. Soon a bunch of kids came up from the lower portion of the school. They were all yelling my name and pointing up to my hiding spot. Behind them was Fr. Schaffer, the parish priest. I could hear their voices crystal clear.

"Right there, Fr. Schaffer. He's right up there."

Jesus Marie, guys. I mean, you goad me into this, and then you turn me in? Fr. Schaffer took me into the office, beat the crap out of me, and called my mom. She had to pay for the window and apologize for her shitty little kid.

Candy Bars and Soda Pop

At the age of about fifteen, Freckles decided to take his mother's car out for another spin while she was spending the night at the Oregon Coast with some friends. After promising her several times that I would behave while she was gone, I took the car about fifteen minutes after she left with her pals. I wasn't worried as I was an experienced driver already—well, sort of. I had driven a friend's car a few times.

I drove it downtown to the pool hall and got some friends. Then we decided to drive through a really rough neighborhood in Portland's northeast district. The area was mostly black and poor. There were gangs everywhere. Although this was not a place for a bunch of white kids to be, there we were—five angry juvenile delinquents, none of whom were even old enough to drive legally, and we were zooming down a freeway with Superman at the wheel. None of these kids had a dad at home. Most had been abused like I was. We were a team of pissed-off kids. After a lot of cruising around, we decided to pull into a gas station and break something. We didn't know what. We just felt like doing some old-fashioned destruction therapy. It helped relieve our childhood anger.

Sitting in front of this now-closed gas station was a refrigerator. Before dispensing machines, you could get a cold drink and a candy bar from inside these old iceboxes as we called them when I was little. The refrigerators were locked and chained at night as they were full of what we called soda pop and candy bars. There was also a small cardboard box in them for change. During the day, when you were getting gas, you could open the door, grab a pop or a candy bar, and then toss in some change. Then at night the refrigerator was locked in a number of different ways. Some gas stations would use hinges with a clasp and paddle locks. Others would use link chains or tow chains with locks. This one had a chain wrapped all around the unit and locked up tight. We decided to try to slide the chain off. We turned the unit on its side and worked at it. After using a crowbar and all the muscle we could get out of a bunch of skinny kids, we managed to get the chain off and had ourselves a feast. I must have drunk about half a dozen Cokes and eaten several candy bars. I was on a real sugar high as were all my buddies. We took some for the road and headed to our next great adventure.

I don't know why we thought we were so invincible. I guess it came with being a testosterone-filled boy growing up. Not only were we the only white people within about two square miles, but also the windows were down, and we were screaming our heads off with the car radio on high. Ironically, we had no idea we were attracting any attention. As we pulled out, I noticed a cop car across the street with two police officers in it. Being a good Catholic boy, I waved at them with a big smile. Oops! He and his partner had been sitting there when we pulled into the station in the first place. The two of them were just sitting there, eating their lunch at 2:00 a.m., when a car of screaming kids pulled up. We ended up being a lunchtime event for them. They just laughed and ate their sandwiches while we entertained them with our crowbar while getting the chain off. When we got pulled over, I did not have a driver's license or any other ID. I was told to get out of the car, which I did. However, before I could even be handcuffed, I took off running. Although I was a freeman for the moment, it was not a bright thing to do. There I was, a tall, skinny, white kid with gobs of freckles and a mop of bright-red hair, running through Portland's African American neighborhood in the middle of the night. I looked like Ronald McDonald running through Watts in the dark. About two hours later, I had run all the way to the Columbia River and was crossing the I-5 Bridge in Vancouver, Washington. Suddenly, the light bulb finally came on. *Duh, they got my mom's car, and they are probably going to figure out who I was. Way to go, Ron.*

The walk all the way through North and Northeast Portland and down across the Willamette River into Downtown Portland took me about three hours. Sitting just two or three blocks from the river was a sign on the side of a large and old Portland building: PORTLAND POLICE DEPARTMENT. I managed to push open one of the heavy glass doors and started walking down all those long and dark halls, trying to find someone. There was no front desk in those days. Finally, an officer walked out of an office.

"Can I help you, young man?"

"I think you are looking for me."

It didn't take him long to figure out what was going on. It was all over the old-fashioned police car radios that some stupid kid had run off after leaving his mother's car behind. After being arrested, I was transported to the Donald E. Long Juvenile Detention Center in Southeast Portland.

Sitting in a tiny room with the door locked really did me in. I cried half of the night. Finally, on Sunday afternoon my mother had returned home. There were no message machines in those days, so she had no idea where I was. On Sunday evening the police finally got ahold of her. I was to go before a judge on Monday, which happened in the early afternoon. My mother had to take a cab to get her car out of the tow yard and pay a hefty fine to the Portland Police Department. On the way home she yelled at me the whole way and did not talk to me again for over a week. I had never seen her so mad, and I did not blame her. At the ripe old age of fifteen, I was charged and convicted with "Larceny of Candy Bars and Soda Pop." The only humorous part of the whole thing was forty years later when I was working for the Oregon State Department of Corrections. About a year after I started there, they found out about it, by looking in our juvenile records. I was the laughing stock of the whole prison. Even the inmates were making fun of me. My new nick-name there was "Candy Bars and Soda Pop." How embarassing. But I still loved the attention.

Tabor East and Tabor West

A little later I started hanging out at two big apartment complexes in Southeast Portland. They were called Tabor East and Tabor West. They were just a few blocks apart. Every Saturday night they would have these huge beer keggers. Many young people like me got into these gigs. It was easy. You just gave them a few bucks at the door, and you were in. Everyone was drunk, and no one cared how old anyone was. They had the strobe lights, a band, kegs of beer, and dancing. Although I wasn't much for drinking yet, I sure had fun with all the noise, girls, and music.

I got there by a lot of strategic planning and hard work. First, I would almost always go to bed early on Saturday nights, telling Mom I was tired. I mowed lawns and did other yard work almost all day on Saturdays and probably was a little tired. But I wasn't about to miss those cool parties. Soon after I went to bed, my mom did likewise. Soon after she went to bed, I would climb out the window, zoom down the ladder, and run through the woods, across our cousins' front yard, down some concrete steps, and I was free. From there it was only about three blocks to the road into Portland. I would walk and hitchhike. An hour or two later, I was in heaven, surrounded by about a hundred or more crazy drunks. What a great life. After a couple of hours of fun, I would repeat the trip in the other direction. Then it was up the ladder and into bed. The final step would be to replace the extension ladder back in its place before Mom noticed it leaning up against the house, below my bedroom window. By the way, all this would not have been necessary if those damn wooden floors in our house didn't creak so much. I could have just walked out the door and back in again. Spiderman had to zip down the ladder, and Superman had to fly like the wind to get all the way across town to the parties and back home again later.

As the old expression goes, "All things must end." Sooner or later my "Tabor East and Tabor West" days had to end. One night at the apartments, I decided it was time for me to make the trip home. I think it was around 2:00 a.m. It was raining out, and I was a good ten miles from home. I stood by the door and asked people leaving the party for a ride into Downtown Portland. Eventually, an older guy said, "Sure." Then he grabbed two bottles out of a case of beer belonging to some arrogant guy who was too good to drink out of the keg. He handed me one, and we were on our way. I always carried a Boy Scout knife on me as I did a lot of hitchhiking. Right after I got the Boy Scout knife, I was kicked out of the Scouts for smoking. At least I got a good knife out of the deal. The guy giving me a ride was looking at me kind of funny, so I put it in my right pocket where I could get to it quickly. In the car on the way to Portland, I was watching this older guy trying to watch me and drive at the same time. He wanted me to come over to his place and party. I told him I had to get home, but his right hand was slowly creeping toward my leg. I am not sure how far he would have pushed it, so I kept my right hand on the door handle and a beer bottle in the other hand to hit him in the face if he touched me. What he didn't know was that tonight's menu would be "Runnin' from the Cops." He had no idea what was about to happen, and he wasn't going to like it.

When I finished the beer, I opened the car window and tossed the empty bottle straight up in the air. I heard the sound of broken glass and smiled.

The open hand creeping toward my leg suddenly turned into a fist. He hit me squarely in the cheek.

"You little jerk! What did you just do? Didn't you see that cop car behind us?"

"Uh, no, I didn't."

Suddenly, red-and-blue lights were flashing, and a nasty siren started blaring. He pulled over and swore he was going to kill me. Two cops got out, and each walked up a different side of the car. My door was opened, and I was told to get out. Seeing that I was just a kid and noticing the older guy at the wheel, I was asked if that was my father. I told him no. Then the officer wanted to know who threw the glass beer bottle out of the car. Being the good and honest Catholic, I told the truth. I was taught from the earliest of days that honesty was paramount.

"He did it," I shouted as I pointed to the driver. "He threw it. I'm too young to drink. I told him not to do it, and look what he did to me. He punched me in the face."

Then I told the cop on my side of the car that he had picked me up hitchhiking and wanted me to come home with him. I told him that I was scared of the guy. Actually, that part was true. The cop on my side of the car told me to go sit in the back of the patrol car while he and his partner talked to the driver. I walked with my head down toward the cop car, still whimpering a bit for effect, hoping the cop would let me go. Passing the front of the police sedan, I noticed a lot of broken glass in the radiator grille. My flying beer bottle landed in the front of their radiator and shattered. The guy I was riding with drank a lot like all of us at that party. He might have been weaving a bit as he was both drunk and spending too much time looking at me. The police probably noticed and were following us. Then someone threw a bottle at them. *Time to pull these guys over.*

When I got to the back door of the police car, I looked forward. Now both officers were on the driver's side of the car. I had another one of my brilliant ideas… *Run!* Just as I was zooming past the car I had been riding in, I threw a big Irish grin at the cops. The one who bought my phony act now had this horrible grimace on his face, and his posture started changing. Suddenly, he was in a sprinting position, but there was no way he would ever catch me. Or so I thought. My bony, little frame helped me move like a locomotive downhill. As I had about half a block on him, I started running my mouth, something I had always been good at. I called him every name in the book and shouted out that I was the one who had thrown the bottle out the window. This guy was fast—I mean, really fast. I don't ever remember losing a footrace. However, there is a first time for everything. He was so close, I could almost feel his breath. I realized that my shoes were part of the trouble. They were clumsy, and I needed to get rid of them. I veered to the right and kicked off both shoes. I was now running through a cemetery and was spreading out the distance between me and Officer Whatever-His-Name-Was. About a minute later, he was closing the gap as I was getting tired. I wanted to call him cheetah as he could move like one. Then I felt the tug. He had me. His hand firmly grasped my jacket collar.

"Gotcha!"

As he began pulling me toward him, his voice was triumphant.

"Got your little ass."

Then terror struck me. This would really suck. I was in a lot of trouble. Just as we were almost at a complete stop, I had something to say myself.

"Okay, okay, you got me. I give up."

The cop was panting so hard, I thought he was going to pass out. His grip on my jacket was solid iron. Then it hit me. The jacket was a piece of crap. Why not let him have it? So I did. As we slowed to a walk, I just slipped my arms out of the coat sleeves and took off again. He was so out of breath and so stunned. He just stood there. About a block away, I turned, and there he was, a block behind me, still panting. I flipped him the bird and laughed out loud.

Rain was pouring down, and I had run about a mile now. I could hear sirens coming from what seemed like everywhere. The streets were lined with asphalt, concrete sidewalks, and buildings. There was no place to hide. I was screwed. Then there she was, the most beautiful thing I had ever seen—a yellow cab with the motor running, waiting for the next customer. I waved at the driver and ran toward the cab. But he almost didn't let me in. There I stood soaking wet from head to toe. I had no jacket and no shoes. My face was beet red from all the running. I was breathing so hard, I almost couldn't talk. To make things worse, all I had on me was one dollar, and I asked him how far it would take me. He was not interested in wasting his time for a buck and let me know about it. The Irish bargainer in me jumped out. I remembered the movie *Oliver,* where the pathetic-looking little boy held up his empty bowl and asked for more. I pretended to be Oliver with the best British accent I could come up with. Instead of food, I needed a ride.

"Please, sir, I need a ride."

It didn't work. He told me to get lost and put the car in gear. Then I tried the truth for a change.

"Wait, I was at a kegger, and I'm underage. I am running from the cops. Please, just a few blocks."

The cabbie was a short, little, bald guy with a soft-looking face. He smiled, probably remembering his youthful days.

"Get in. A buck will buy you a ride across the bridge."

Thank you, God. If I make it home alive, I will say five Our Father's and ten Hail Mary's. I will even go to church two weeks in a row. On the way across the bridge, I began telling him the whole story. You have probably already figured out that I am a good negotiator. Many members of my family were insurance salesmen after World War II. It was a good way to make a living if you were a good talker. I had learned well from my parents and grandparents that a good story could keep your audience in their seats. What I needed was a longer ride for my buck. When I got into the part about the beer bottle landing on the grille of a cop car, I had the taxi driver by the you-know-what.

"So where you goin', kid?"

I kept talking, and he kept driving. Before you knew it, we were three blocks from my home. I thanked him and got out. I am sure he laughed all the way back to Portland and then some. When I got into bed and fell asleep, I kept having nightmares of the angry cop. He was probably still looking for me. At least I let the driver off the hook. He surely got a DUI, but at least he didn't get busted for the beer-bottle incident. That was my last trip to Tabor East and Tabor West. I really miss those parties.

The El Camino

There I was in my hot El Camino and my new girlfriend, Lydia. I was twenty-three years old and already owned a motorcycle shop. Life was good until I opened my mouth.

"You ever outrun a cop?"

The young lady paused, not knowing what to say. It might help to understand that her father was a recently retired concertmaster at a prestigious New Jersey symphony. They had moved to Portland, Oregon, where her mother became the principal cellist for the Oregon Symphony for twenty-five years. As for Lydia she had graduated from a fine East Coast college and would become a librarian and fourth-grade teacher in the Portland area for many decades. Then what was she doing with this guy who, although in his twenties, still had a juvenile-delinquent streak. I had been in the Army for three years and was going to college part-time. Although I would later graduate more than once in the years to come, this poor girl had serious reservations about me. We had met on a Saturday night and dated for the next sixty-two nights. Within three weeks, I had asked her to marry me. To my surprise she said yes—the biggest mistake she ever made.

"No, I have never outrun a cop."

Thinking that she had missed something fun, I decided to treat her to the experience. A few minutes later I saw a police officer a couple of cars behind me. My El Camino had a vicious 396 V8 with about four hundred horsepower under the hood. I put my foot into it right there in Downtown Portland. As expected, the officer took off after me. The following few minutes looked like something on the *Dukes of Hazzard* except Daisy wasn't amused. Noticing the claw marks from her fingers forming on my dashboard, I decided, maybe this wasn't a great way to get a girl. I spun around a couple of corners and ditched my ride in a parking lot full of cars. An old Portland furniture store was having their annual warehouse sale, and the place was packed. I sat there in the car with a big grin on my face as the police car sped past the parking lot without seeing us. Lydia wasn't impressed. I apologized and decided I would only do that alone in my car or on one of my motorcycles in the future. While a rational person simply wouldn't do that, I was not a rational person. That would come later in life. Somehow that poor woman still sits across from me at the dinner table nearly five decades later. I am forever grateful for that. I am a changed man, on the outside at least.

The Great Meier & Frank Robbery

I was playing pool at my old after-school hangout when I saw them. One day I noticed two straight-faced-looking men in black suits with white shirts and ties. To say these guys looked mean would be a total understatement. They just stood there in the middle of Wayne's Billiards Academy in Downtown Portland, Oregon, staring at me. Their faces were like cold statues, and I was getting worried. Not even an eyelid moved. Finally, I got really scared and decided to leave. I was six-feet-one-inch tall and weighed one hundred twenty pounds. If you blew hard enough in my direction, you might just knock me off my feet. In motion I looked like a piece of wet spaghetti wobbling back and forth in the direction I was walking. The only thing I could do was outrun them. But there was just one doorway out, and these two guys who looked like descendants of J. Edgar

Hoover were standing in the way. Hopefully, I was just imagining things, and they were a couple of office workers checking out the pool hall. Soon they would walk away, and I could breathe a sigh of relief. *Keep believing that, Ron, and you might find some oceanfront property in Arizona.* I took a deep breath and walked toward the stairs, down to the front door. One of the two guys in suits stepped aside and let me by. At the bottom of the stairs, I turned and looked up. Both of them were staring straight down at me like two vultures eyeballing a piece of roadkill.

A couple of weeks earlier, I quit my job at the Meier & Frank department store. I was a salesclerk in the sporting goods department on the sixth floor. The store had been in business since the early 1900s and was a well-established business in Portland. The store was bought out by Macy's in 2005. The job was really boring, and at eighteen years of age, I wanted more excitement. I had flunked out of a Catholic college and was just hanging out, living with Mom. *As far as the lust for excitement, be careful what you pray for, Ron, as you might get it.*

At a lunch break from the store in a nearby park, I found myself sitting next to a man I had seen there before. He was in an army outfit. After a few minutes, he addressed me.

"I noticed you sit here at lunchtime every day, eating by yourself. You looked bored. Would you like some excitement in your life?"

I did not tell this man that I already had some new excitement in my life. It was upside down. I had lost my driver's license because of several tickets and had just been caught the second time for driving without a license—not bad for a guy who had only been driving for a year. My mother made me wait until I was seventeen until I got my driver's license, because she thought I wasn't mature enough at sixteen. Mom insisted I would be more grown-up and responsible at seventeen. Fooled her, didn't I? She should have made me wait until I was forty. My driving troubles along with all the other juvenile delinquent behavior had landed me in court. Standing in front of the judge with my head down, I prayed he wouldn't find out about my stealing Mom's car, pending larceny charges and a couple of things I did during my short three-month stint in college before being expelled. *Please, God, I need leniency.* My attorney told me I would be doing some jail time. I was devastated.

But the Vietnam War was in full swing, and our country was looking for troops. Lucky Ron was about to find a way out he had never even thought of himself. I had tried one term in college and had flunked out. I was bored at my job and basically directionless with the future. I was a convicted juvenile delinquent and criminally insane driver. I was hopeless.

So there I was standing in front of the judge, waiting to be given the death penalty. Suddenly, I thought I heard that forgiving and loving Catholic God speak to me. The judge asked me to look him in the eye, which I begrudgingly did.

"It looks to me like there isn't much hope for you, is there?"

I was so scared, I couldn't even fake tears. The spunky little, red-haired, and freckle-faced boy was out of words and excuses.

"No, sir, I am a mess and guilty on all accounts."

The judge fell silent for what seemed like an hour However, it was probably more like sixty seconds.

"I am going to give you a choice, and I hope you make the right choice. You can go to jail, or you can serve your country. What is your choice?"

I was so shocked that I didn't understand what he meant. *Serve your country?* All I could muster up was that I didn't want to go to jail. The judge told me I had thirty days to enlist in the military. I was told that it was useless for the court system to continue their efforts in changing my behavior and that he hoped the US military would have better luck.

I wondered what the guy in uniform meant by excitement in my life. One thing was for sure. It was a complete and total conspiracy. How could it not be? I screwed up life, and a judge gave me one month to sign up and serve my country. Then a day later this military recruiter is sitting next to me on my lunch-hour break. How could that be? Once again, I was being led by something a whole lot bigger than me. I just accepted it and was glad I wasn't going to be locked up behind bars.

That was all it took. I followed this guy, who was an army recruiter, to his office a block away. I signed a few papers, quit my job, and went home to tell my mother what I had done. She would miss me, but she was also glad to be done with this out-of-control kid. She really hoped three years in the army would help me. Mom was right. The military straightened me out a lot. The following day, I went straight to Wayne's Billiards Academy and told everyone I had joined the army. I shook a few hands and headed down the stairs and out the door. Suddenly, I noticed the two guys in suits standing in front of me.

I do not remember which one of those guys in the suits grabbed me first, but it hurt. So did the handcuffs. Somewhere in there I heard a last name follow by "FBI." I was devastated. My friends and the pool-hall owner, Tony Wayne, rushed over to see what was going on. I was escorted out of the building and taken to the local FBI headquarters in Portland. I was drilled for a couple of hours and told that I was guilty of robbing the Meier and Frank store and that I would be spending about ten years in prison. I was then told to go home, get an attorney, and wait until I would be dragged through the trial of the century. At least it would be for me.

The very day I left my job at Meier & Frank to join the army, someone at Meier & Frank robbed the place. There were just over one hundred cash registers throughout the ten floors of merchandise, and each register had exactly one hundred dollars in it. At the end of the day the register would be emptied of the day's sales, and a hundred bucks in change and small bills would be put back in to start the next day. As this job required a register key, it thus had to be an inside job. There was only one security person at night, and it was decided that the thief had figured out how to maneuver from floor to floor as the guard moved around on his nightly route through the store. Also, it was determined that the thief hid in a bathroom stall when the store was closed for the night. Then they went about the business of stealing ten thousand dollars, one cash register at a time. That was the Great Meier & Frank robbery of 1966. Thank God, it never made the newspaper as my good Irish Catholic mother had already suffered enough with all my juvenile-delinquency episodes over the years. I think the store wanted to either wait until someone was caught or just avoid the embarrassing press coverage. I said nothing to my mother about the whole affair. Surely, the great superhero Ron could pull this off. I could hide the whole affair from her with ease. Right? Wrong! Two days later, the car that I rode to the FBI office in, with handcuffs on, was parked outside our home. The same two guys got out of the car, stopped me in front of the house, and started drilling me again.

"So you signed up for the Army a week before you robbed the store. That was clever. The recruiter says you signed up to go overseas. Were you planning to hide the money in another country?"

I almost burst out laughing. I mean, I was a little juvenile delinquent, yet I was also the guy who mowed lawns and had a paper route—you know, the skinny, little kid with red hair, freckles, and zits? Now I was the mastermind of some huge heist? After a short, but very uncomfortable discussion in our driveway, I went inside the house to face my mother. I had no other choice. I had to tell her the truth. She was stunned. I tried to calm her down and laugh it off; however, the woman who taught me how to laugh at everything was now worried sick.

When I went to bed that night, I peeked out the window, and there those guys were—just sitting in that four-door big, black car, smoking cigarettes, and drinking coffee. *Wow! These guys really think I am the robber.* I didn't sleep much that night. Thankfully, they were gone in the morning when I got up. Before I left for the Army, I found out they had interviewed some of my friends and neighbors. After that, they did not come back. They just left me in limbo. Days later I went to the army recruitment center with a small bag. I went to basic training for six weeks, spent eight more weeks in advance infantry training, and was sent to Korea during the Vietnam War. There was a little fighting in Korea at that time, however, it was nothing like what the poor guys in Vietnam went through.

Three years passed, and I came home. Weeks later, the same agents showed up at my house.

"So what did you do with the money? Did you bank it overseas?"

They drilled me for a few minutes and told me that they knew I did it. I was a felony robber and had gotten away with it so far, or so they thought. I protested to no avail. They were determined to prove that I was the bad guy they were looking for. They walked away from my mother's house and never came back. The truth be known, I was a small-time delinquent kid, not a felony robber. I wondered for a long time if they ever found the guy who did it.

To make things worse, I discovered that when you left a job to go into the military, the company was required to offer you a job when you got back. I had started back in school full-time at Portland Community College. I wanted part-time work, so where do you think my first stop was? Meier & Frank. My old boss was still there, and I spoke to him. He called me a criminal who got away with robbery and promptly told me to get out of the store. I went to the personnel department where the hiring took place. A man there told me they had no work for me. I told him that he was required to give me my old job or an equivalent job. I also told him that I was not the infamous Meier & Frank robber. I said if I was, I certainly would not come back and ask for a job. He thought for a minute and made a phone call. I waited for security to come and escort me out. To my relief, they didn't come. Instead, a gruff-looking man with an unlit cigar came in and told me to follow him. I thought maybe he was a maintenance manager or something like that. I figured I might be mopping floors. To my surprise, I spent the next couple of years working part-time in the Meier & Frank parking lot. I actually enjoyed parking cars and working in the cashier's office. I stayed there while going to college.

Mount Angel College

Just prior to my job at the Meier & Frank Company, I tried my first attempt at college. About five months after my father's death, I had graduated from Jesuit High School, just west of Portland, and was ready for college although I wasn't sure if the college was ready for me. They had no idea of the mistake they made in accepting me.

And they would surely come to regret it. Mount Angel College was a quaint small Catholic college about forty-five miles southeast of Portland. Set in the farm and wine country, the college was about five or six blocks east of the town of Mount Angel, which was only about four blocks long itself. It looked like something out of a Norman Rockwell painting. It really was one of the most beautiful and most peaceful places on this earth—until I showed up.

I don't think I had been there much more than a week when I made my presence known to the police. I had a little money saved up from mowing lawns and other odd jobs that summer and decided to buy a car. I bought a 1947 Chevrolet that had been T-boned on the passenger side for twenty-five dollars. This was in the fall of 1966. It had been hit so hard that the passenger side was seriously caved in, and neither of the doors on that side opened. My college buddies didn't care. We would all just pile in on the driver's side, and off we went. The muffler had a huge hole in it and was really noisy. To make things worse, the car smoked really bad, and the engine had this terrible knock. We were sure it was the crankshaft. Fortunately, we only had to drive a few blocks from the school to downtown Mount Angel, so we didn't care if it didn't run very well. We just kept pouring oil into the engine and ignoring the knocking. About two or three days after I bought it, a Mount Angel cop pulled me over for a loud muffler. When he asked me for my driver's license, I lied and told him that it was back at the dorm. Before he let me go, he told me to get the muffler fixed or get that car out of town. I was informed that if I drove it through town again without getting it fixed, he would arrest me and tow the car to the junkyard. What he didn't know was that I didn't have a license. It was suspended for three years for a string of tickets in Portland over the last year.

I drove off intending to do absolutely nothing other than drive it right back through town the very next day. However, that evening one of my classmates said that the cop was parked behind my old Chevy in the college parking lot. He had a pad and was writing things down. Then he left. Sooner or later he would run the license plate and find out it was not registered to me and that I had a suspended driver's license. The next day was Friday, and the weekend was upon us. My friends and I devised a highly sophisticated and brilliant plan. We would drive the car as fast as it would go through the Main Street of these four-blocks-long so-called town. Somehow the cops would magically not hear it, and we would take it to Portland and drop it off there at a friend's house.

The speed limit in this little village was twenty-five miles per hour. About five thirty after school and an early dinner, we decided to implement our great plan. Besides, the police department only had one jail cell. Surely, they wouldn't put all of us in there, would they? After we fortified our stomachs with some alcohol, off we went. We were truly on an adventure. Or so we thought.

While it was not actually the car from the movie *Back to the Future*, the old Chevy still had some guts to it. As we passed through Mount Angel, the speedometer read somewhere around fifty. Maybe we could outrun the cops after all. *Good luck with that one, Ron.* To our surprise, there were no cops on the one and only street through this thriving metropolis. After a seven-mile drive to a little, but much larger town named Woodburn, we were still laughing and scream-ing with delight. We had beaten the cops—well, at least one officer anyway. He was probably having his dinner at the one and only café in Mount Angel and did not want to leave his chicken and fried steak with mashed potatoes to get cold while he chased a carload of drunken college students. No matter what the reason, we felt like a bunch of really bad thugs. I mean, we had devised a plan, executed it, and got away with it. Life was good.

Thereafter we continued to drink beer and drive north on an old highway. It was not a freeway—rather, a four-lane highway that wound its way through several small towns on the hour-long trip to Portland. Somewhere on this road one of my friends now informed me that he no longer thought it was a good idea to park the car at his parents' house. It looked like a small tank that got blown up in WWII. Most of the windows were broken out or cracked. It was painted about three different colors, and the body damage was not limited to the passenger side. There were dents and scrapes every-where. Even the front grille was knocked out, and the trunk had a big dent in it. Besides the awful paint job, about half of the car was rust, and all four tires were bald. I mean, what do you expect for twenty-five bucks? Even in 1966 that would hardly buy a good bicycle, let alone a car.

So now that we could not take it to my friend's house, what were we going to do with a pile of junk car? The only thing we knew for sure was that we could never take it back to Mount Angel. It was a Friday night, which meant we had all weekend to get rid of it. Back in Mount Angel that officer would be looking for both me and that car. When he found it was missing from the college parking lot, there would be hell to pay. He did not have to be a detective to know that if it was not in the parking lot, this would mean someone was driving it. That would be little Ronnie Weber, and he would be on the lookout for me. How hard was it to find someone when there was only one road going through a town of only a few hundred people? He would park on that road and wait. Ronnie would come, and he would get arrested. *Get out of the car, Ron, and take the bus back to college on Sunday.*

Driving north later that evening, I thought we could just stuff it somewhere and come get it later or, better yet, leave it there for good. After arriving in a little town named Tigard, we decided to switch roads over to a larger town named Beaverton, about five miles west of Portland.

Suddenly, the engine started to knock louder than before. Smoke was no longer coming out the exhaust pipe. In the midst of our sophisticated escape plans from Mount Angel, we forgot the car needed oil. Now there was no oil in the motor, and the engine was letting us know. We were on the corner of Cedar Hills Boulevard and Canyon Road when the knocking signaled the toll of death. I decided, the only thing I could do was run. Then I thought of an even better idea. Why not just blow it up? I would drive it as fast as it would go until the engine would blow up, and that would be that. The guys all thought it was a great idea. I turned right on Canyon and put the pedal to the floor.

We had driven the car forty miles from Mount Angel at no more than twenty-five miles an hour as the clunking was so bad and the car was so damaged, it was awkward to keep it on the road. I do not know how we got it as far as we did. By the time we had gone about half a mile, we were now doing at least sixty miles per hour toward Murray Boulevard. The car was weaving all over the road, and the motor was knocking so bad, it sounded like a machine gun on a B-24 bomber.

About five blocks east of the junction of Murray and Canyon, I heard this huge explosion. I immediately yanked the steering wheel to the right to get over to the side of the road. The car had other ideas. With the motor completely frozen up and the drive wheel locked, the car slid on the bald tires. We dropped down into a ditch on the north side of Canyon and smashed into a muddy bank. One of the guys in the car was a mechanic and said we had thrown a rod right through the engine block, and our ride to freedom was over.

The beer had run out at least an hour earlier, and we were all cold sober. We were also frightened by what had just happened and didn't want the cops to see us. Being the cowards that we were, we responded quickly when a guy in the back seat hollered, "Run for your lives."

We managed to walk about five miles and got to my mom's house. Dad had passed away, and my two older brothers and sister were either in the service or at college. My mom was living in the huge house we grew up in all by herself and was glad to have some company. In the morning, she started asking questions. She wanted to know why a handful of college freshmen showed up sopping wet at midnight, and as there was no other car out front, she wanted to know how we got there. After telling her some lies, she made us breakfast. Soon after, I told her we had homework to do and needed to get back to school. She was happy to give me the money for bus tickets and dropped us off at the Downtown Portland Greyhound Bus Depot. I believe she knew we were up to no good and now wanted to get rid of us quickly.

A few hours later we pulled up to the Woodburn Greyhound depot and hitchhiked the seven miles back to Mount Angel as there was no bus service there. A couple of days passed, and I was leaving a sociology class with not a care in the world except which girl at the college would get a chance at the greatest guy on earth. I mean, how bad could a guy named Freckles be? Suddenly, I heard a voice behind me from the curb. When I turned around, there he was—that big cop. And of course, he wanted to see the title and registration to the car as well as my driver's license.

Now I have never been the smartest guy in the world, but I was a damned good liar as a kid. I also knew that cops weren't stupid and didn't like people who acted that way, especially when they weren't. I had to act quickly, so I did. I looked him right in the eye and told the closest thing to the truth that I could come up with. I simply told him that I was brokenhearted because I went to Portland to see my darling Irish mother and the car broke down. I continued telling him that I must have been cheated by the guy who sold me the car as the damned thing didn't last hardly a week. I explained that I would now have to be walking everywhere, and all the girls would ignore me as who wanted to date a guy in college without a car. The cop stared at me for a moment and appeared to be either dazed or speechless. He looked disappointed as, I think, he really wanted to arrest me for something. I knew for sure that if he had been anywhere near the Main Street on Friday evening, I would already be handcuffed and in the back of the car. However, I was still worried he would get me for something. Surprisingly, he showed a compassionate side and said he was sorry to hear about the car. He figured, without a car, I would be walking around town from now on. Without another word, he got in his car and left. I believe he knew I had gotten away with something and would be keeping an eye on me. I vowed not to give him the chance although that probably would not happen.

A week later I found something even better than the college girls on campus. It was a 1954 Packard Clipper. It was parked a few blocks off the eastern edge of town, inside an old barn. The door was open and I could see the car. In the front window was a small and hard to read sign. I walked closer and saw that it said, "For sale." It sort of looked like the owner really didn't care if he sold it or not. There was not even so much as a scratch on it. The car had an immaculate interior and all the power equipment available in a car at the time. The windows were power as were the seats and also the antenna. Even though it was twelve years old, it was really a sweet-looking car.

Then I knocked on the door of a house next to the barn and asked the owner the hard question about pricing and nearly fainted when he only wanted fifty dollars. I was so stunned, I asked him why it was so cheap, and he told me it had not been started in about two years. It was his wife's car, and she had passed away a couple of years back. He did not want to sell it as she had bought it new in 1954. He also could not drive it either as it reminded him of her not being in the car with him. He also didn't want to take the trouble of trying to sell it. It just sat in the barn all that time and did not run. The tires were low, and the car was covered with dust. I knew it would run and look great with a wash and a polish. I bought the car, and my friends helped me clean it up as well as install a battery. Within a couple of days, it looked like the Starship Enterprise to us and was on the road. However, it had one problem. It had a huge engine and went very fast.

All these years later, I do not remember what size the engine was; however, I do know it was the biggest V8 available at the time. It accelerated like a jet airplane in combat. The first day I brought it on campus, a girl whom I was in love with snubbed me once again. Being stubborn, I was not going to go out without a good fight.

"So, Carol, do you like Packards?"

"What?"

"Packards. You know, the big luxury cars. Do you like them? I have one in the parking lot. It is right there. See, the big, gray one right out front."

"Oh my gosh! That's your car. Really? Can I have a ride in it?"

While we were driving through the parking lot, a few of my classmates saw us. Their dazed looks made me feel like king of the world.

"Ron, what are you doing in that car?"

There was nothing else a good little Catholic boy could do other than tell the truth. If I said I paid fifty bucks for it, that would not sound cool. Some poor old farmer gave it up for pennies on the dollar because of a broken heart. The car was worth way more than that. I told them my rich grandmother gave it to me. She was always spoiling me with stuff like this. Then I gleefully rolled up the power window, gave a honk from a horn that sounded like an incoming freight train, and drove off with the hottest chick in the college. I was in heaven. Carol gave me a dirty look, knowing I had bought it for fifty dollars from an old farmer. Then she laughed about it.

Alas, I had forgotten that there were no liars, thieves, or juvenile delinquents in heaven. I had snuck in the pearly gates without St. Peter noticing and would soon be caught. When we drove into Mount Angel, Carol promptly wanted a milkshake to go. She wanted a ride in the country with Cool Ron and his great car.

On the way out of the hamburger joint, with two milkshakes, I noticed something very big standing in my way and tried to move around it. It moved too. It also had a blue uniform with a bright and shiny brass badge midchest, on the left side. It was my policeman friend again. Lucky me.

"Nice car, young man. Where did you get that? It looks like Old Man Miller's. When his wife died, he parked it in the barn. A lot of us locals had our eyes on that car, but he wouldn't sell it. How did you end up with it? Did you steal it?"

I told him about my lucky find and was promptly asked how much I paid for it. I knew he would probably shoot me on the spot if I told him, so I lied.

"I think I got robbed. I paid him four hundred. He was a nice guy, however, I sure had to pay a lot for it."

The officer looked satisfied and walked away. You know that feeling when you are about to die, and you get out of it briefly for a moment or two? Yeah, that one—sort of like the deer-in-the-headlight look. He knows he is going to get hit, but just stands there staring at the oncoming headlights. Somehow, I knew there would be hell to pay, and I just wanted to get away from him. He scared the crap out of me. So I just told that awful lie and got away. Carol seemed impressed. Little did she know, there also was the driver's-license issue. As the officer had never gotten any ID, car title, registration, or driver's license from me on the old Chevy, I thought he might not even know my name. Why didn't he ask me for the paperwork and my license? There were a lot of rich kids at this college, and maybe he was treading carefully. I was thinking that if he ever found out I was a fatherless kid, it was all over for me. I would be headed for the tank.

Carol and I drove away with our milkshakes in hand. She was thrilled, playing with the power windows and enjoying the nice afternoon ride in the country. We stopped at a little rest place and watched a creek go by while we finished our shakes. Then it was time to make the move. I just had to kiss her. Unfortunately, I remembered she had a boyfriend on the football team. If I touched her, he would beat the crap out of me. She noticed me looking at her with lust on my mind. She said I was a nice boy, and we could be friends. My angel wings started melting, and my stomach began to hurt. Time to go back to the college and tell everyone I did not get to first base and hope her boyfriend didn't kill me. Little did I know that the fun had only begun. Just when you thought things couldn't get any worse, you found out different.

On the way back I was feeling disappointment. She was so cute I really wanted to kiss her, but that would never happen. With a dark cloud over my head and a bad mood creeping up my backside, my musing was suddenly interrupted with the sound of an old-fashioned siren. Shit! There he was, in my rearview mirror, lights flashing and siren blaring. His face looked like he had a big smile on it too.

After I pulled over, I heard those ugly little words.

"License and registration, please."

Oops. Even Superman could not get out of this one. Then he spoke again.

"Fifty dollars? You said you paid four hundred dollars. Old Man Miller said he let you have it for fifty bucks. Why did you lie to me about it?"

This time it had to be the truth, the whole truth, and nothing but the truth. I told the officer that I knew I had gotten the deal of a century and did not want anyone to know it. I was afraid someone would accuse me of cheating the old guy out of his beloved and dead wife's car. That was not what happened, and I told that to the cop. I asked the old guy what he wanted, and he told me fifty bucks. Still, I wanted to keep it a secret. If felt nice to drive a fancy big car, and I wanted people to think I was rich too. The officer seemed to understand that. I also surprised him and actually did tell him the whole truth. I informed him that my license had been suspended in Portland; however, I thought it would be all right to drive a car to and from the college in this really small town. Then I got ready to be arrested. I didn't really care as my attempt at seducing Carol had failed, and I was totally deflated like a serious flat tire. Then the officer surprised me.

"As you do not have a license, I am going to have to tow your car to the police impound lot. As for you, you and your friend are going to have to walk back to the college. See if you can stay out of trouble. As far as your car is, get your license reinstated, and you can have it back even if you did steal it."

As he walked away, I could hear him mumbling about how cheap I got it for. I was also shocked that I was not hauled off to jail. Then I had to walk all the way back to school, listening to Carol go on about what a loser I was. All I could do was think about that car. In fact, the next day I decided to go see the officer and try to work out some kind of deal. I stupidly thought that maybe I could pay a fine and get the car back. *Bad idea, Ron.* However, I could not easily lose my fascination with that stunning automobile.

When I arrived at the police station the next morning, I did not even go inside the tiny building. I just went out back to where the towed vehicles were stored and decided to have a good cry. Sitting in there were a couple of old beaters that were not worth claiming and a couple that were marginal. As I scanned the lot, I saw nothing else. I walked around the police station, and my car was nowhere in sight. I was really confused. I went back to school and said something to the guys. We were all wondering about it for the next few days. Then an older student heard about it, and I was told to talk to someone in town who might be able to help. I did and soon was taught one of life's hard lessons. I was told that I would not be charged for driving without a license again and that my car was gone. Nothing was ever said about it again. All these years later, I still wish I had that car. I am sure that cop still has it in his garage at home.

Now you would think that after only two months in Mount Angel and all the trouble I was getting into, I might have the slightest inkling to grow up. Well, actually, that would come later. I wasn't done yet. I had one more thing to do before I was kicked out of the college.

Somewhere between Halloween and Thanksgiving, a bunch of us guys decided to have a party on a Saturday night. This sort of fell under that old saying, "The best-laid plans of mice and men." The trouble was that my plans were usually not the best ones made.

We decided to have a panty raid at 3:00 a.m. Now a right-minded young man would have left it alone—I mean, run into the three-story girls' dorm, make a lot of noise, grab some panties, and run out the door. Then again, Freckles was never a right-minded person. He used to like another old saying that went something like this, "Dare to be different."

Walking through town earlier that evening (because I no longer had a car), I noticed a small farm behind the college. Another student had told me it belonged to the college. The Catholic nuns ran the farm, which had a garden. There were also some small farm animals too. Out back the nuns had an old, green pickup truck. My brilliant idea was to borrow the truck and fill it with small animals (chickens, goats, and anything else we could get our hands on). I saw a small pig and did not know if it was a baby or one of those pigs that was genetically small. I grabbed it too. We got it into the back of the truck and drove about a half mile to the girl's dorm.

Somehow, in our drunken madness, we forgot how much noise we were making, especially with the animals. We drove up onto the grass and parked in front of the building. The idea was to get as many animals into the building as we could before waking anyone up. We figured the commotion of all the animals and frightened girls running around would give us the chance we needed to see who could snag the most panties.

If you are starting to get the idea that Freckles is going to complicate things, you are on the right track. I decided to outdo the competition and take the little pig up the elevator to the third floor. However, by the time I got up there, most of the female students were already out of bed. Girls were running all round, screaming as the moment the first of the chickens were let loose on the first floor, the noise had aroused nearly every female student in the building. As the elevator door opened on the top floor, the pig ran out squealing.

I don't remember if I had another girlfriend by that time although I kind of doubt it. The word was out that Freckles was not a good bet for the young Catholic women looking for a future husband. Still, I did not want half of the student body seeing my face. Right outside the elevator door was a fire-alarm pull switch. I followed the pig out of the elevator with my hands hiding my face as best as they could, turned, and pulled the alarm.

Suddenly, no one was interested in the animals. Now everyone was running down the stairs. I ducked down in the middle of a bunch of girls and ran down the stairs with the crowd, hoping nobody would see that a boy was in the middle of a fleeing mob. The trouble was that it did not matter if I made it down unnoticed or not. A dorm nanny of some sort (a Catholic nun) had called the police the second she heard a pickup truck come crashing over the curb and drive across the nice green lawn.

When we all funneled out the front door, there was a fire truck and the entire Mount Angel Police Department, consisting of about two cars and two or three officers. And as foxy as Freckles thought he was, he could not get out of this one. There he was, standing at six-feet-one-inch tall in pants and a shirt, surrounded by dozens of short, young women in pajamas, nightgowns, and robes. Bad Freckles.

This time I would spend the night in another dorm in Mount Angel—the jail. The following morning, I was taken to the edge of town by an officer and let out of the car. I was told to never come back. I walked and hitchhiked until I got home. It took several hours. A week later I was back at the school, sitting in the dean's office with my mother, a few nuns, several stern-looking priests, and of course, the college president. It was over quickly. I became the first Weber since my forefathers arrived here in 1850 to be kicked out of a Catholic college. I was a complete disgrace to my entire family. My mother cried, and we left. I never went back there.

CHAPTER 5

THE MILITARY: TOWER GUARDS AND DOBERMANS

There comes a time when most people grow up. Sometimes it is ten, twelve, or maybe sixteen years old. I was a slow learner and did not hit that mark until about nineteen. The drill sergeants knew right away that I was a little smart-ass, always trying to be funny and look-ing for the attention I rarely ever got at home. Basically, they just physically beat the hell out of me enough times to where I finally stopped being a little boy. I became a respectful man in the military whether I wanted to or not. It was about time. After basic train-ing in Fort Lewis, Washington, I was sent to Fort Ord, California, for advanced infantry training. I also know that I was sent to AIT because I was going overseas.

I was in Korea during the Vietnam War (1967–1969). While we were not in an active war like Vietnam, constant incidents were happening. I was stationed at Camp Casey, where atomic bombs were stored. The North Korean soldiers would occasionally try to slip through the fences in an effort to either steal the bombs or just blow them up in place. It would have been a huge embarrassment to the United States, so the bombs were secured carefully. I was a tower guard, and my shift was from 11:00 p.m. to 7:00 a.m. The towers were about twenty feet up in the air and open to the whole world. I was a sitting duck as were all the other tower guards. Fortunately, there was a cease-fire agreement, but it was still scary because North Korean soldiers (NKs) were always breaking it. At night during the winter, the low temperature was typically around twenty to thirty degrees below zero with high winds. Calculating both the cold and the wind gave us a chill factor of around thirty-five to forty degrees below zero during the coldest months of the year.

The North Korean soldiers would attempt to cut through our fences to wreak some havoc or just to scare us. I was only nineteen years old and terrorized by their insults, rock throwing, and the like. I remember one night when it got really bad. I was a new tower guard, and the NKs knew it. I called the sergeant on the radio and asked for help. A few of the North Koreans appeared to be cutting through our fence while yelling threats at me. Some were pointing rifles at me. Fearful of restarting the Korean War (1950–1953), the Department of Defense issued strict orders, "not to fire unless fired upon." This was mostly due to the unpopularity of the Vietnam War at the time.

After radioing for help, a gravel-voiced sergeant answered at my end of the radio. I was abruptly told to "fight like a man" if the time came. I was only nineteen years old and had never been in a situation like this. It was so frightening that I remember peeing on myself.

Also present in my mind were the eighty-three crew members of the American navy ship the *Pueblo*, who had recently been kidnaped by the North Koreans (January 23, 1968). We were all deeply heart sickened about these poor men who were being tortured day and night by angry North Korean soldiers. One of the captives was killed by the North Koreans. Most of us could hardly sleep thinking of what was happening to them. All we wanted to do was break into North Korea and rescue those guys. However, this would cause unwanted attention at a time when Americans were sick of war. Consequently, those guys spent twelve months in hell before being released after exhausting negotiations between North Korea and America. The *Pueblo* ship would be kept as a tourist attraction for North Koreans, a total humiliation for us. It was just one of those things we never forgot.

That night in the guard tower, I was just plain paralyzed with fear. Whether the NKs were just taunting me or whether they were seriously trying to break through the fence, I didn't know. That night, I was beginning to understand that up there in the tower I was easy target. I needed a backup plan. I decided to climb down to the ground and use some of the small shrubs around the tower to hide behind. In the daytime, these small bushes would not have been of much help. In the dark, things were different. Between the darkness and fog that night, they might just have saved my life.

About 3:00 a.m. I could hear what appeared to be bolt cutters snapping their way through the cyclone fence. I got down on my knees, pointed the rifle in a northern direction, and waited. I prayed like never before. I also had backed up twenty feet from the base of the tower to put a little more distance between the North Korean soldiers and myself. I was also really worried that not staying in the tower might set me up for "dereliction of duty" charges. I was not allowed to leave the tower although I would rather be in a military prison than be dead. The truth was, I had only been at Camp Casey for a very short time and really did not know what the hell to do. While trying to be the kind of solder America wanted, I also was preparing myself to retreat, if necessary, in order to stay alive. So basically, plan B would be to fire a couple of shots and then run like hell. However, I also knew that this might just be harassment on me as a new tower guard.

Suddenly, I heard a lot of foot traffic. I thought the NKs had gotten through. However, I quickly determined that all the new commotion was coming from behind me. I turned and could barely make out what looked like a cloud of dust coming at me through the darkness. It was approaching really fast. Directly in front of me I heard a bunch of loud, yelling NKs and could only see what vaguely resembled human figures running north. Why were they suddenly running away? The noise behind me increased to the point of driving me back to the guard tower. I did not want to be caught on the ground.

When I stood up, I noticed that all my rescuers were only about waist-high. What did the sergeant send—a bunch of pygmies? They were also not yelling as you might expect charging soldiers would do. Whatever were approaching were making growling noises. Suddenly,

I remembered seeing a canine unit on the first day I arrived at Camp Casey. *Go, Fido.* However, now I began to realize that I might have a bigger problem than I did in the first place. Yes, the troops were here to rescue me, and yes, the North Koreans were running back north; however, did these dogs know the difference between the enemy and me? *Hey, guys, I am an American. Please don't bite me. Our Father who art in heaven…*

The dogs were about a couple of dozen or more. They looked like an even mix of German shepherds and Dobermans. *My, what big teeth you have.* The bad news now was that they were only about forty yards from me, and the gap was closing very quickly. The good news was that I was nineteen years old, six-feet-one-inch tall, and about a hundred and thirty-five pounds. In other words, I was fast. I ran like the wind to the tower and climbed up as fast as I possibly could. I think there were only about two inches between my feet and those snarling snouts as I pulled myself up to the platform twenty feet or so above them. The dogs hit the fence so hard that I thought they were going to push it all the way into North Korea. The canines were making such a fuss that I didn't think those North Korean soldiers stopped running until they were in China.

Sometime after this, I learned that the North Korean soldiers were not really cutting through the fence that night. They really did not want to get into another full-blown war any more than we did. However, they were ordered to harass us by their commanding officers, and they were just doing their job. Meanwhile, my radio was going off.

"Weber, where the hell are you? Answer me, goddammit!"

Shit, I had left the radio in the tower when I left my post. I finally grabbed the radio and managed to mutter something like, "Thanks, Sarge! I'm okay." The sergeant was actually just coming up the hill from the base. All was well. Or was it? I looked down at the dogs, and there was my rifle on the ground. Now I was really in trouble. At this point I did not care if I got bit. Down the ladder I went. I slowly worked my way through the snarling dogs and their huge, shiny teeth. *Nice puppy. Nice little puppy. Please don't tear my arm off.* Once the rifle was in my hand, I ran up the ladder as fast as I could.

When the sergeant pulled up to the tower, he came up and asked questions about the situation. The last question was, "Were you down on the ground?"

Now any right-minded, dishonest guy like me would do no better than be honest at a time like this. But, I would be sent home with a dishonorable discharge or on my way to a military prison. Besides, I didn't think this sergeant made it past the fourth grade. He had a heart the size of a lion, but a small brain. So I lied.

"No, sir. I was not."

When he told me that he thought he saw a taller figure than the dogs on the ground, I simply told him that I threw down a snack for the dogs as a reward for saving my bacon.

"It wasn't me, Sarge. Swear to God. It must have been one of those dogs jumping up to get half of a sandwich I threw down for them."

Sarge gave me a funny look and left. While I was in Korea, we had two barracks blown up with multiple casualties and injuries, the hijacking of the *Pueblo* navy ship with eighty-three personnel on board, a US Navy plane shot out of the air, killing thirty-one passengers, and the Blue House raid, which terrorized South Korea for eight days. Thirty-one North Korean commandos were killed in that attempt to kill the South Korean president. In addition, scores of North Koreans were always trying to cut through the DMZ fencing. It was a constant battle to keep them out, especially on the eastern DMZ. While we were not officially at war with North Korea, a lot was going on. Forty-three Americans lost their lives over a three-year period in that time, which later would be called the Second Korean War. It was also called the War that Almost Was. One hundred and eleven were injured. The only thing that slowed it down was the constant pressure from American citizens to get us out of Vietnam. Demonstrations and riots were breaking out all over the United States. Actress Jane Fonda and many other well-known Americans were leading the charge to bring our soldiers home. If the public had found out that dozens of American soldiers had died in Korea and that there was still fighting going on over there, it would have been a public-relations disaster. The media was silenced.

During those nights in the towers, I felt deep sadness for the folks in Vietnam. Fighting, for many of them, was a daily or weekly exercise. It was a living hell that those of us who were sent to Korea in the late 1960s were able to avoid. Our rare skirmishes were peanuts compared to what Vietnam vets went through.

My Korean Girlfriend

When we landed in Korea, it was the first time I had seen Asian people up close. I was raised in a complete and total white society all the way through grade school, high school, and my first attempt at college. I was never even near people who were black, Asian, Hispanic, Middle Eastern, or any other race except white. Today I am amazed that life could have been that way. We are now in the 2020s, completely integrated with people of all races of the world, and I enjoy it. When I got off that plane in the summer of 1967, all I saw were thousands of Koreans. We white American soldiers were a huge minority. We were surrounded by a race of people we had never seen before. We lived in barracks with KATUSAs (South Korean soldiers), ate with them, worked with them, and even went to the bars in the villages with them. On weekend nights we would go to the bars, drink, and look at the girls. At first I didn't like the girls. I thought they were not very pretty. After a while, things were different. Being so lonely over there, five thousand miles from home, all it took were a few beers, and they started looking a lot better. One of the worst parts was that we had never been acquainted with the food they ate. Their mainstay was a dish called kimchi. Kimchi was a fermented cabbage dish. Although it tasted good to them, we hated it. There were two kinds of kimchi—winter and summer. It was made stronger in the winter when the temperatures would drop to twenty degrees below zero. Though it helped the Koreans stay warm, the odor was really strong. When the girls wanted to dance or just sit and talk to us, we could really notice it. Sometimes we got mad and called them kimchi breath. Overtime we just adapted to it. We also learned to adapt to them singing. They tried pitifully to sound out

American songs. While they kept trying, they still sounded terrible. Because we were so homesick and lonely over there, we enjoyed the music as best we could and threw a few bucks on the stage when they were finished for the night.

I quickly learned that the girls on the streets and in the bars wanted to do something more than talk, sing, and dance. The village outside Camp Casey was something I had never seen before. There was no electricity in the homes. A few bars had a couple of light bulbs strung from the ceiling, and that was about it. The people lived in little concrete rooms. A whole family of several kids all lived in rooms no bigger than a bathroom we have in our home here in America. There were no bathrooms or anything else—no running water to drink or bathe in. There were no beds or mattresses. They just slept on the concrete floor with sparse blankets. Small chunks of coal were shoved under the concrete and lit to warm the concrete they slept on. Food was prepared with little coal stoves. If you needed to go to the bathroom, you just walked outside where there were ditches lining the muddy streets. You just peed or bent over to defecate right there on the street with people walking by. Big trucks with suction pumps would suck out the urine and poop every week or so. The human waste was used as fertilizer for the nearby cabbage fields. How these people survived was beyond me.

A sergeant told me one day that the only income the Koreans in that region had was us. They lived off the money earned at night when the GIs went to the villages. You could buy drinks, food, T-shirts, trinkets, and girls.

The whole thing made me sick. I mean, I enjoyed drinking, talking, and dancing; however, the girls wanted money from us for sex. Their breath stank, they smelled bad, and they were just skin and bones. While they needed the money, I just couldn't bring myself to do it. Oftentimes I would just give them a few dollars and leave.

One night, a tiny Korean man stopped me on the street. He had noticed I was telling the girls to leave me alone.

"You no like girls? You want boys? I get you boys."

I told him I liked girls, but what were available were disgusting, diseased, and stank like pigs—not to mention the kimchi breath. Then he said, "You come my house. I show you."

Show me what? I thought. Out of curiosity I went anyway. I was curious. Their house was a room about half the size of a small American bedroom. The floor was concrete. The rest of it was made of scrap wood and metal just thrown together. If it had not been leaning against another building, it would have fallen down. However, the place was clean. Clothes were hung up, and next to two chairs was a mattress, which was a rare commodity in that village. Next to the one room was another really small one with another mattress that took up the whole space. It was like a second bedroom or something. It had its own door to the outside. On the floor of the bigger room they had was a brood of filthy little kids and a sickly-looking mother. He pointed to the kids and told me I could have any of the boys or girls I wanted. They cost a dollar each, and I could do whatever I wanted to them. I almost threw up at the idea. With no intention of hurting any of those children, I handed him some money so he could feed his family and left. Lying, I told him I would think about his proposal. I quickly left to never return.

Arriving at my barracks almost a mile away, I told some of my fellow soldiers about the awful experience. They told me not to worry. It was simply a rental proposal. But I had never heard of such a thing. My fellow soldiers told me that if you offered the father about a dollar a day, you would have a clean, disease-free girl (or boy if that was what you wanted). You got the little side room, which was also heated by coal burning under the concrete floor. While you were abusing their child, the parents kept the coal burning and gave you a bowl of rice each time you came. There were a few pieces of rat, cat, or dog in the rice because they knew Americans liked meat. There were no cows anywhere near this village, so there was no beef.

Although I could not stomach the whole thing, I would go to the village for some entertainment. It beat lying on my bunk in the barracks. The father of those children kept following me around for days, repeating his offer. The guys at the barracks kept telling me how lucky I was to get such an offer. It was considered an honor.

While the families were starving, they didn't want a bunch of different drunken American GIs with their kids every night. Venereal disease was rampant. The girls liked the idea of a regular customer, kind of like a boyfriend. I also couldn't bear to imagine what the children went through to get money for food and clothing for their family. I also wondered how hard it was for the parents to sell their children. That night in the barracks one of the guys told me that if I made an arrangement with this father, I would be feeding and clothing a whole family. That hit me hard.

The following night, I went back to the father and complained about the ages of the children. He told me to wait. I just stood there staring at those poor children. They looked at me with big eyes, never saying a word. I knew, either they hated me or they were praying for me to take one of them so their family could eat. What I didn't know was that the father had an older daughter. He kept her working in the bars. He was hoping I would take one of the younger kids, and then they would have two incomes coming in. Bringing me his older daughter meant there would be haggling about how much I was willing to pay for her, because he would only have one girl bringing money in. While I was waiting, he was searching for his daughter in the clubs. A few minutes later he brought her back. Although she appeared older than the rest, she still looked young. He told me she was eighteen, but I wasn't sure I believed him. One thing for sure was that they looked younger than their actual age because of a lack of food. Maybe she was eighteen after all. I would also soon learn that by the time the girls were about twenty, they were no longer marketable. Girls who worked the bars had sex with over a hundred guys a month—sometimes a lot more. By the end of a single year, a girl as young as eleven or twelve would have had sex more than a thousand times with hundreds of different men. By the time many of them were in their early twenties, they were either dead or sick from venereal diseases.

The older girl had pretty good English skills, and I sat down with her alone. I wanted to know how she felt. She just kept saying she would be a good girl for me and make me happy. With fear and desperation on her face, I could see the tears coming. She was scared and confused. Her father slapped her for crying. At that point I stopped him and said I would take her as she was and pay him thirty dollars a month. His whole family would benefit from this. They would have food, clothing, and respect in the village. It was a happy day for all of them. The average income of a family in American money was anywhere from ten dollars to a hundred dollars a year. There was very little money exchanged because most families there didn't have any. They bartered and traded for rice or material for clothes. Things like soap was a rich person's commodity. That was why most of the girls didn't smell good. Having American cash was like striking gold. Thirty dollars a month was three hundred and sixty dollars a year. This was way over the average income in that village. While hard-working girls in the clubs might earn more than that, they were often sick with VD and had other health problems from so much sexual contact. A girl might have sex five to ten times a night with different men. When she had a regular steady, then she would have sex once a night with the same man. She also got two nights a week off and was not allowed in the clubs. If she got caught cheating, the man could drop her, and the contract was done. As a regular steady income was important to the family, the parents made sure the girl wasn't fooling around for extra money. So having a regular was a lot safer for both the girl and the GI.

What the hell had I just done? All I knew was that her name was Sung Lee, and she was considered my personal property at that time. I didn't know what I should do next. The girl knew exactly what was supposed to take place. She immediately pointed to the little room and the bed. I let her know that I wasn't ready for that yet. Instead, I took her to the bars. I explained to the father that I was not interested in having sex with her at this time. I just wanted to have a friend and nothing more. He got confused about it, so I told him some hard truth. His English was good, so I was able to tell him straight out that I was not going to crawl in bed with someone who might have venereal disease. The girls in the bars were given VD tests weekly on Fridays. If they did not have any VDs, they were issued a card that indicated this. If they did, they had to go to a medical facility and get treated. Until they were clean again, they had to work the streets.

Most GIs knew better than to touch them. It was the drunken soldiers they preyed on.

All I wanted to know was that Sung Lee was clean. The father was okay with that. Although she was disease free, I was not sexually attracted to her yet. I just wanted a companion. Although it was hard for her and her father to understand that, we got through it. Sung Lee and I walked all over the northern regions of South Korea, and she told me all about her family, country, and life in general. I fed her like a pig, and after about three or four months, she began to look halfway decent. I bought her clothes, junk jewelry, and a few other things. I think she was the only person in the village that had Crest toothpaste and a brush. Normally, you had to be drunk to be with a girl because the kimchi smelled so bad. After a few months and a lot of grooming, she began to look like a young woman, and life took its course from there. I had taken on a project, and it really helped me pass my time over there. The family was looking a lot better. The kids had meat on their bones and clothes on their backs.

One of the deciding choices of how I handled all this was being dragged out of bed in the middle of the night. It scared the hell out of me. About five American GIs woke me up and pushed me outside. I thought I was going to get my ass kicked. But that did not happen. They woke me up to see what one of them called the "dead man walking" buses. I stood there, freezing cold, and saw all these soldiers being wheeled out in chairs or carried on stretchers. Some were walking with crutches or just very slowly. What was clearly evident to me was that they were all very sick. When I asked what was going on, the guys in my unit told me that they were American soldiers who were so seriously infected with venereal diseases that they were not going home. They were going to a camp in Japan where they would die from those infections. Their lives were over in their late teens as a result of their poor choices over whom they slept with. They were loaded into one bus, and then all their belongings were loaded into one or two other buses, and off they drove. The guys did this to me so I would understand the importance of being careful about going to the village and jumping in bed with any girl they saw. All new recruits got the same middle-of-the-night wake-up call that I did. I didn't sleep a minute for the rest of the night. I also stayed with Sung Lee for the rest of my time in Korea. There was no hopping around for me.

I spent over a year and a half in Korea and never got VD. I really fell in love with that girl. I thought she was ugly-pretty, and she teased me constantly. She had never seen a white man with red hair and freckles. I was six-feet-one-inch tall and hardly weighed much more than she did. I barely passed the army physical to get in the service. I was really skinny. We both did a lot of growing up while I was there. When I left, she was about a hundred pounds and healthy. The whole family was too. The younger kids had nice clothes, and they had plenty of food. All this was from my paycheck. What was going to happen when my tour in Korea was finished? It was really hard for me to leave. Both she and her parents wanted me to marry her and take her back to the United States. I did too, but sadly, they could not find a birth certificate, and the military would not let me take her without one. My heart ached for Sung Lee for a long time. We had carved out a little niche of happiness in this desolate place so near the Korean DMZ. Somehow in one of the worst places in the world, two totally different people found joy together. The pressure from her parents to marry her was on, because after I left, the family would drop back into poverty. The parents even tried to talk me into marrying her and leaving her there, which the military said was okay as a civil marriage held in the village had no connection to them. The parents said they would find a birth certificate and send her to America later. A military chaplain told me it was just a ruse to get money out of me. I would be living in the States and sending money to a girl I would probably never see again. Sung Lee was scared and brokenhearted. I was completely devastated. The last night, we both just stood there staring at each other. I dropped my gaze to the floor, turned, and walked away. The girl ran after me, holding on, yelling, and crying. Tears were running down my face. I dragged her all the way to the main gate of the base. Two MPs pulled her off me, and I walked into the compound. She hung on the fence surrounding the base and begged me to come back to get her and take her home with me. Neither of us had ever been with anyone else. While I was even begging myself to run back and get her, I knew I couldn't. We were just worlds apart. I cried all night long. The next morning, I got on a plane back to the United States. I would finish my time in the service, go to college, marry, and have children like all my friends. To this very day, I still wonder what happened to her. I hope she found another guy soon so she could feed her starving family. I hope he was nice to her. I hope he married her and took her to America. I really do.

Friendly Fire

Friendly fire is usually referred to as when we actually shoot or otherwise injure one of our own, normally by accident. However, this time I am talking about something slightly different. It is nearly getting killed or beaten to death by your own troops in other ways. Usually, it is when a fellow soldier goes berserk and goes after the closest person. Our Quonset hut had about sixteen soldiers in it. There were two blacks and four South Korean soldiers, and the rest were whites. Sometimes it got a bit heated in there. We had to be careful about whom we pissed off.

Not long after I got to Camp Casey, Korea, I went to Tongducheon, the local village. I went there on weekends mostly. Normally, I would go straight into the center of the village where most of the clubs were. This night I decided to go to the right. I had never gone this direction before. I walked about a quarter of a mile out of curiosity where I saw a large club with live music. That was really rare in Tongducheon as there was very little electricity available at that time.

When I got to the club, I noticed that the lights were out except near where the band was playing. The dance floor was full of soldiers and prostitutes. Even though no one could see much in the dark, it looked like everyone was having fun. I found the bar and grabbed a beer. Soon I was on the dance floor having a great time myself. Suddenly, something hit me and knocked me down. I assumed it was just an accidental elbow from another dancer. I got up and kept dancing. Pretty soon I got hit again. This time it was a hard fist that landed on the back of my head. I went down like a ton of bricks and almost passed out. I struggled to my feet to see who hit me and to kick his ass. However, I wouldn't be kicking anyone's ass that night. I got hit again, and before I could get up, people started kicking me. I felt like I was going to pass out as I couldn't get free of the mob on top of me. Finally, a big, black man, who was a cook at my unit and slept in my barracks, pushed himself into the crowd and started shoving people off me. He grabbed me and dragged me out of the club, yelling at me all the way. Even though I was beat up so bad and could hardly walk, Willy told me to get the hell out of there as fast as I could. A crowd of blacks had started gathering outside the club. They could not believe some white guy just walked into their club. I mustered all I could get out of me and began holding on to anything I could while I walked away from the club. Some of the shop owners were giving me nasty looks as I crawled back to the front gate. The military police saw me and helped me into Camp Casey. They wanted me to go to the hospital, but I refused. I felt pretty embarrassed about the whole affair. They called a jeep for me and took me back to my unit. The next morning, I was black-and-blue from the top of my head to the bottom of my feet. I never went back to that side of the village again.

The next morning Willy really let me have it. I was told that I was in the wrong side of town. Only black people were allowed there. In that dark club I didn't even notice I was the only white guy in the there. It was 1967, and segregation was pretty common. I was not familiar with that. I had never been around any black people. They were not allowed in my Catholic schools or anywhere near my rich white neighborhood. We had live-in help, and they had to be white. Not being around any other people than white my entire life, I just never experienced any form of segregation. However, I sure did that night.

Willy slept in a bed in our hut just two bunks over. He was always a great guy who was friendly to anybody, white or black. As he was a really big guy, no one ever got smart with him although he was just a big teddy bear at heart. Thank God, he was in that club that night. I don't think I would have lived through that experience.

One of the worst situations in my tour on the Korean DMZ was not with the North Korean soldiers. It was in my own Quonset hut. I had gone into the village one Saturday night. Weekends were really wild and a lot of fun. That night I had a bowl of rice at one of the clubs. Although there was always a suspicious-looking little meat in the rice, I paid little attention to it. As I was eating, I suddenly noticed two Korean civilians running down a small hill in the back of this particular club. They had a long pole between the two of them, resting on their shoulders, with a howling dog tied upside down in the middle. I was so surprised, I said something about it to some of the guys sitting at our table. They all started laughing, and one of them said, "What do you think you are eating...beef?"

By this time, my face turned red, and I stopped eating the rice with the mystery meat in it. The laughter went on for about five minutes. I was told the meat in the rice was dog, cat, snake, rat, or anything else they could find. There were no cows within fifty miles of Camp Casey. I don't know if it was just my own head or what when I started to feel a little sick. I went back to the base. Truthfully, I think I was just embarrassed. When I got back to my unit, there was no one in the Quonset hut. It was only around 9:00 p.m., and everyone else went to the village except for the South Korean soldiers. They hated the prostitutes and wanted nothing to do with them. Every night after dinner they would go outside and practice tae kwon do. They were really good at it. My Korean friend Kim was a sergeant and in charge of the South Korean soldiers in our unit. He was a grandmaster in martial arts. Sometimes when I saw him, I would immediately jump into a martial-arts position and threaten to kick his ass. Eventually, he got the idea and started laughing about it. I would come at him, and he would run back a bit, pleading with me not to hurt me. We had a lot of fun with that. He was a great guy, and I would have stood next to him in any combat situation.

That night I just took a shower and went to bed. I was asleep by ten. While I was sound asleep, I suddenly felt my whole head on fire. Whatever hit me felt like a freight train. As I tried to gather myself, I was hit several more times. I was thrown on the hard concrete like an old rag doll. I was still half-awake and trying to understand what was happening. I thought whatever hit me had broken every bone in my body. I was bleeding and completely beaten to a pulp. Before I could figure out what was happening, I heard Kim and his friends yelling, and all of them grabbed a great big GI off me. It wasn't easy as the guy was a ten-year veteran of the military and a seasoned martial-arts expert himself. I hurt so bad, I was sure I was going to die. Kim beat the hell out of the guy and came to my aid. He and his soldiers put me in a jeep and took me to the hospital. If it weren't for them, I would have died that night.

After a trip to the hospital, I learned that the guy who attacked me was someone from our Quonset hut named William. He went berserk that night after a girlfriend ran away with some money of his. He had been in the Army for a decade and was still a private like the rest of us. He hated that as he had been in long enough to be a sergeant. He drank a lot and was always in trouble. He was demoted several times and was mad about that. Sadly, he was also one of the ugliest men I had ever met. He couldn't help it. He was a poor kid from the South, and life had just not gone well for him. The Army was all he had. What shoved him over the brink on that Saturday night was a horrible mistake he made. William had reenlisted for six more years and received a huge reenlistment bonus of ten thousand dollars. In the 1960s that was one hell of a lot of money. He had a girl in the village whom he liked although she didn't care much for him. She was glad to take his money for sex, but that was all. However, when she heard about his big money bonus, she told him she wanted to marry him. He fell for it and gave her the ten grand. They were supposed to be married the following weekend, and when he showed up, she was gone, and so was his ten thousand dollars. He came back to our unit that night drunk on his ass, and there I was asleep in my bunk. He took out all that anger on me. When I was asked if I wanted to press charges on him, I declined as I felt so sorry for the poor guy. Now he had ten more years to serve and not a penny to his name. I was surprised he didn't hang himself on a showerhead.

Months later in the village, a fight started between GIs and Korean citizens. What had happened to me before led me to tae-kwondo lessons. I was getting pretty good and just wanted to protect myself from all the violence. However, this fight was not going well for the GIs. There were a lot of Korean men who were martial-arts guys, and we were losing. Suddenly, a couple of Korean men zeroed in on me. They were running right at me. I prepared for the worst. Then about ten feet from me they stopped and backed up. That was when I noticed what looked like a grizzly bear standing next to me. I turned my head, and there was William, the guy who lost it and kicked the crap out of me. This time he was on my side. He kicked one of the guys in the face so hard, he went down on the ground and did not get up. The other guy took off running.

The military police soon broke it up, and William walked me home. Although not much was said on the way back, it didn't need to be. In the silence, I knew he didn't mean to take his anger out on me a few months before. I forgave him, and that was the end of that. Oddly, we became friends after that.

One humorous event happened about two weeks after I got to Camp Casey. I had asked some of the other soldiers how I could say something nice to one of the girls in Korean. Two of the fellow soldiers taught me how to say, "You are a beautiful young woman." I practiced over and over every morning and night. I would stand in front of the mirror in the bathroom and repeat the Korean phrases over and over. Finally, the big day came, and I walked out of the front gate into the village. Young prostitutes were lined up trying to get money from us GIs. It was the only way they could make enough money to live.

I stood there a bit confused as I was a newcomer to all this. I did not want to take a prostitute to bed although I would pay her to go to the bars and dance with me. So there I was, ready to show some pretty girl how I could speak Korean. I opened my mouth, and out it came. I said what I had practiced so hard and then bowed. I was really proud of myself. But instead of her smiling and thanking me, she kicked me square in the balls. Immediately following were several punches to my face. Before I knew it, I was on the ground. Looking up, I saw her turn and yell something in Korean to a crowd behind her. At that point several of her friends ran up to me and kicked the crap out of me. This was when I first met the military police for the first time.

Within seconds of my wonderful speech to the young lady, the MPs were dragging the women off me. They pulled me up and rushed me to the MP office at the front gate. By this time, rocks were flying at us. Once we were safe, one of the officers asked me what the hell happened. When I told him what I said to her, the three cops started laughing really hard. What my fellow GIs in my unit told me to say to her was not "You are a beautiful young woman." Instead, it was a bunch of really bad things. I had called her an ugly fat bitch and a few other things. The joke was on me, and I was the only one not laughing.

Not long after this a guy in our hut told me that he wanted to show me something. He had noticed I was shy and not really interested in the girls other than drinking and dancing. He decided he was going to make a man out of me. I had an uneasy feeling about him as he was pushy. His name was Bob, and he was a first-class bully. I mean, he was just trouble. I didn't want to go, but some of the other guys were going, so I joined them. Everything was fine until we got to the village. Most of the guys went into the normal clubs. Bob decided he was taking me and one other newcomer to a part of the village I had never seen before. We walked down a long dirt road to a small structure. He knocked on the door, and a woman with two young girls opened the door. Bob spoke crystal clear Korean. After they talked, the woman left, and the two girls stayed inside. Bob started yelling at them, and they started crying. He wanted them to dance naked, and they wanted no part of it. They were too young, and it looked like they had never done this before. By this time, I was getting really uncomfortable and told him I wanted to leave. He slapped me across the face and told me that he was doing this for me. He thought it might get me excited, like a warm-up exercise before we went to the bars for prostitutes. Then he went after the girls, who were crying hysterically. They weren't doing what Bob wanted, and he was mad. When he slapped one of the girls, I ran out the door.

The parents were right outside. I started yelling at them to go in and get those girls out of there. They were too damn young. I handed the mother a little money, and she went into the house. She and Bob started yelling in Korean. Finally, Bob and the other GI came out. The woman started screaming at Bob for money. He pushed her away, and then the father came, and Bob knocked him down. By this time, I was half a block away. Suddenly, a rock hit me in the back. A mob of Korean adults were coming after us, throwing rocks. I just ran as fast as I could and got back to the gate. Bob and the other guy were right behind me. For weeks after that I was sick to my stomach. I had never seen such depths of poverty before and how desperate people were when it came to starvation. They would even sell their own children. Although I promised myself that I would go back there and give that family some more money, I never did. It was just too dangerous. As far as Bob was concerned, I let him know that I was not interested in his friendship. He was a sick pedophile, and I wanted nothing to do with him. He threatened to kill me if I told anyone about that night. He left me alone after that. I am in my seventies, and I still see those two little faces. I can still hear them crying. They will haunt me until I die.

One day near the end of my tour in Korea, I was told I would be going to Vietnam. I went to my sergeant and asked about it. He told me that because I had a secret clearance, I could extend my Korean tour, and he would help me do it. It wasn't so much as going to Vietnam that was bothering me as it was doing two overseas tours back-to-back. So I stayed in Korea for several more months and finished my tour in the military at Fort Hood, Texas.

When I came home from Korea, I still had about a year to go before I would be discharged from the Army. Other than a few bar fights, things were pretty calm. I had a job in a supply unit. We just handed out what anyone needed, like uniforms, bedding, boots, and other necessities. On weekends I would rent a motel from Friday night to Monday morning. I was really tired of cramped barracks and Quonset huts. I was tired of the fighting and all the violence in this world. I would spend the weekends in almost total silence. For as long as I have lived, I will just never understand why there has to be so much anger and hate in this world.

The Gay Bar and the Smashed Corvair

After three years in the Army, I returned home, ready to get on with my new life. The juvenile delinquent was gone. There would be college, marriage, kids, careers, and a lot more. First, I wanted to visit some old friends and hangouts. One was Wayne's Billiards Academy, my old hangout in Downtown Portland. I had only been home three days, and I drove my Chevrolet Corvair convertible. I had bought it outside Fort Hood, Texas. There were many convertibles in climates like that. But I lived in rainy Oregon. Why in the hell did I buy a convertible? It was probably because I would have an afternoon paper route. Between showers, I could take the top off and throw the papers all the way across the yard and up to the front door without ever leaving my car.

So there I was, the veteran coming back to reclaim my territory. While I was a wimpy little kid when I left, I was now a buff ex-military dude. I was ready to rock and roll. Two blocks from the pool hall, I was hunting for a parking spot. It was really hard, and I was getting pissed. Suddenly, I saw someone a block away pulling out. I just throttled my car to get there before someone else got to it. On a Saturday night, parking spots were rare. This spot was gonna be mine.

Bang!

I don't know if I first felt the impact or heard the awful sound. Blood was running out of my broken nose, and I hurt like hell. When the dust cleared, I saw a gigantic Ford station wagon about three feet from the front of my car. The front of my car was about two feet shorter, and the hood was popped up. As the Corvair had a rear engine, there wasn't much up front other than a thin sheet metal that bent very easily. The driver of the other car was out and yelling at me. As I was totally focused on that parking spot, I failed to see a stop sign on that busy street. I just stood there with a rag on my nose and trying to figure out what the hell had just happened. Twenty minutes later we had exchanged insurance information, and the Ford drove off. Damage to his car was minimal. My car was almost not drivable. A bunch of onlookers helped me to get a parking spot and push my poor little Chevy into it. Soon they were gone, and I was standing there in the rain alone and mad. I decided to go to the pool hall and tell old Wayne my miseries. Surely, he would still be there, and maybe he would let me play on the tables for free after my debacle.

When I went to the front door, it was locked. When I looked through the glass doors, I saw a lot of people up there. I turned south and saw people going into a new entrance. I walked over and climbed the stairs up. When I got to the top, all I heard was loud music, and across the room people were dancing. There was a greeter at the front door. I asked him what was up.

"Where is Wayne's Billiard Hall?"

"The pool hall? That closed two years ago. Wayne moved to Florida. Now there is a nightclub here."

Rats! I was really looking forward to telling Wayne all about my military service. It would have been nice to see him again. Disappointed, I decided to go in and drink my sorrows away. Besides, maybe I would get lucky with some hot chick. "I just got back from the military" was a great line. I sat at the bar and looked at all the pretty colored bottles of booze. After growing up with big parties at our house and tons of booze, I saw what it did to people's lives. I decided to stick to the beer.

The bar was lit up with flashing colors everywhere. Loud music filled the air. I hadn't ever seen anything like this before. Military bases and the small towns around most of them just had dives—I mean, dim lights, sad music, and old people drunk as hell. Tonight, in Portland I was in heaven. Soon I felt a tap on the shoulder and was asked to dance. Now that was really new. I mean, the guy always asked the ladies. Right? I guess not anymore. The gal was tall and cute in an odd way. I hadn't been around American women for three years and was just getting used to it. During my basic and advanced infantry training we were not allowed off the base. Then it was a year and a half in Korea and another year in Texas, where the base was surrounded by Mexican women. So off to the dance floor we went.

With the flashing lights and all the people crowded on a small dance floor it was hard to tell who was dancing with whom. After a few fast dances the band decided to play a slow song. While we were dancing to this music, I could not help but notice how buff she was. Maybe she worked out. I just decided to enjoy the beer, the music, and the new love of my life, whatever the hell her name was. After a while we decided to sit down and talk at the bar. When I gave her my sad tale of woe regarding the nasty car wreck, she started laughing to the point of pissing me off. I asked her why she was laughing at me, and she told me that she worked in a body shop nearby, and she was here with some of her coworkers. She also told me her name was Steven.

The look on my face would have probably sent a grizzly bear running for its life.

"Oh, you're not gay, are you?"

"Uh…"

"Did you know this was a gay bar?"

"Uh… No. I have been away for three years in the Army, and the pool hall that was here for many years is gone. I just came here to play some pool and talk to some old friends."

"Sorry to hear that. Let's go look at your car."

I was speechless for a moment and then found myself walking down the stairs and out the door to look at my car. Steven looked it over and said, "Wait here."

I sat there in my car, wondering what the hell was going on. The wait seemed like an hour. It was actually more like fifteen minutes. Steven emerged from the nightclub with four guys who looked like girls. They all came over to the car and started examining it. Two of them went to their body shop a block away and brought back some tools. For the next several hours they banged, pried, and twisted. All I was responsible for was the beer. I went to a nearby store and bought a case of Bud.

I wish I had taken a video of the whole thing. There I was, sitting on a park bench at 2:00 a.m., watching five gay guys slugging it out with what was left of my car. When it was all done, the whole front end was straightened out. They used Bondo filler and sandpaper to smooth everything out. The front hood was totaled out, and I would have to replace it, get a new headlight, and paint the front of the car. After the horrible accident, my totaled Chevy Corvair was no longer headed for the junk heap. Later that week I went to a place called the Earl Scheib Paint Shop. In 1970 they would paint a whole car for $29.99. I would have to put the masking tape around the lights, windows, etc. myself. I was happy to do that. After a used hood from a junkyard, a new headlight, the paint job, and a couple of other small items, my car looked like new for about a hundred bucks. I told those guys that I didn't know what to say. I thanked them over and over and still felt it wasn't enough. They were okay with just having fun, drinking beer, and helping out a veteran. So we sat there until the sun came up, laughing about all my zany adventures in the military. I will always remember those guys and their generosity.

Oddly, they gave me another gift. I had never been around gay men. The only thing I had growing up was the distaste the Catholic Church had for them. But that night I discovered they were just human beings like me and everyone else. They were born the way God made them. They were so kind to me that night, they could not possibly be damned to hell for being the way they were. Any prejudice I might have gotten from my church and family, growing up, was wiped out that day in the winter of 1970. Also, their gift was a big help to me over fifty years later when a granddaughter came to me five years ago and told me that she was gay. I just remembered my old friends, gave her a big hug, and told Jessica that I approved and loved her. Thanks, guys.

CHAPTER 6

THE CAREER

In the fall of 1972, I wrecked a motorcycle. I had no insurance, and it was trashed. I paid three hundred dollars to a Honda shop for it, and now it wasn't worth fifty bucks. I had bent the front end and the frame. I managed to hobble it home and stuff it in my mother's garage. A few days later I decided to take it all apart and throw it in the large dumpster at a gas station down the street. About halfway through the teardown, I had a thought. Maybe I could run an advertisement in the local paper and sell the parts of the bike. As there were no personal computers or Internet at the time, you had to call the newspaper, and an associate would take your information. You could also handwrite it out and mail it to the paper with a check for three dollars. There were lots of good parts left on this motorcycle, so why throw them out? I ran the ad, and the phone rang off the hook. People were calling me from all over the Portland metropolitan area. In a matter of a few weeks, I had made six hundred dollars.

I really pondered over this. Maybe it was a way to make money. At this time, I had dropped the lawn mowing as well as the newspaper delivery and quit the parking-lot job. The company that owned the parking lot still thought I might be the one who robbed the Meier and Frank store and resented being forced to hire me when I came back from the service. They were really glad to see me leave. Actually, I was kind of enjoying being Ron the Robber. I mean, there was no way I ever did anything like that. You would have to be a major criminal for something like that. I was just a snotty little delinquent and nothing more. After the FBI had come to the pool hall, interviewed my neighbors, and made such a huge thing over the whole matter, practically everyone thought I was a real bad guy. Some neighbors and people at the church stopped talking to me. However, the fun part was that a lot of friends thought I was a successful robber and got away with a huge caper. They sort of respected me. Whenever I was asked about it, I would just laugh and pretend I got away with it. Then I gave them a big smile and walk away.

After my morning college classes, I was working in an import auto-wrecking business. It was a junkyard for cars, and my job was to tear cars apart when they came in. When my boss heard about all the money I made on the sale of my totaled motorcycle, he decided the two of us should start a motorcycle-wrecking yard. It was a hit. There was nothing like it in the Portland area or anywhere in Oregon. We were buying wrecked motorcycles from insurance companies throughout the state. In the past they would have to take them to the auction yards, and they were sold for pennies on the dollar. My boss at the junkyard and I signed contracts with all the major insurance companies in Oregon and Southwest Washington. We would pay a set amount of money based on the size of the motorcycle. We agreed not to cherry-pick, choosing all the best ones and leaving the rest. We purchased all their wrecked bikes. Before we knew it, we had a building full of wrecked bikes, and customers were pouring in the door. It got so busy, we had to move to a new building a few miles away. Three years later I bought a commercial building in Southeast Portland and moved my shop over there. It was on a four-lane extremely busy road, and my income nearly doubled. I was able to start buying rental houses.

Meanwhile, my mother and our friends thought I had lost my mind. My college teachers and fellow students said I was making a big mistake. I was majoring in business management, and some of the professors thought I would go bankrupt in a short time. Even the bank nearly ran me out the door. I had a good friend in the loan department, and he shunned me. He was afraid of getting fired for making a bad loan. I ended up borrowing as much as I possibly could on an old pickup truck and my Chevy convertible. I needed money because six months after we started the business, my boss at the import-wrecking yard sold out his half of the business to me. He was opening up a new salvage yard and needed some money for that. He was the only person I knew who believed I could make the business work. As far as all the naysayers, I just hung in there and fooled them all.

Having a motorcycle shop at the age of twenty-two was pretty damned cool. I had my own business, I made good money, and the girls loved me. I drove hot rods. Mostly, they were the big-block, high horsepowered, and cool-looking. I was still going to college and had a great young manager of the shop named Brent. If you are still out there, Brent, thanks for all you did. We had a lot of fun tearing down wrecked motorcycles and selling the parts. Winters were slow while spring, summer, and fall were super busy.

When big motorcycles came in, sometimes I would fix them up if they weren't too badly damaged. Then I would drive them around for a while. Over about six years, I owned about every motorcycle they had in those days. During my years in the motorcycle shop, I began racing. In North Portland, there was a track called the PIR (Portland International Raceway). The track raced cars and motorcycles. I had also tried and miserably failed at dirt-bike racing. All the hard bouncing up and down were too hard on my back. But I was in love with straight-out speed on pavement. I never made a living out of it because it was too dangerous and sometimes really scary. I rode a Harley-Davidson race bike at close to 130 mph on a straight spot by the bleachers and nearly ran off the track at the first corner. I was trying to make up time as I didn't do well in the corners. I never really won anything. Who cared? I sure had fun.

On another day I lost control at over a hundred miles per hour on the same straightaway. I had what was called a high-speed wobble. The handlebars were flying back and forth so hard, they smashed my hands into the gas tank. I hung on as hard as I could until, about seventy, I went off the track into the grass. The bike was sliding all over the place, and finally, about thirty-five I laid it down. I just threw it over on the right side. I put both feet on the rear swingarm and both hands on the left side of the handlebars. The bike slid a long way on the grass and finally flipped me off. Ironically, I wasn't even hurt. The bike was totaled. I stood up and bowed like I meant to do that whole thing and was just showing off. Then I put what was left of the bike in my El Camino, went home, and cried. I loved that bike. However, with a young wife and two little kids, I was done. I never went back to that track—better to be a coward and live. We were living in a luxury hilltop home with beautiful views. I had seven motorcycles at home, two nice cars, and a big, black, antique Cadillac limousine. I also had some really hot Chevy El Caminos for the business. Life was good. Why risk it? After several years, we sold everything—our home, business, a commercial building, and some rental houses. We built a new home west of Portland and set up a True Value Hardware store.

The Hardware Store

The store was named Weber's True Value. Here we had a second child and lived there for nearly twenty years. Running a hardware store was both fun and hard. I loved being around all those tools and hardware stuff. Although there were a few hardware stores in the area, there was room for all of us. Though the town was small, there was a huge farming community for miles around. We had a few employees, and business was good although there were always challenges. Sometimes an employee might not show up or just be lazy. Overall, most of the workers were great.

One particular man worked in the evenings and drank a lot. He kept a bottle in the storage area at the rear of the store. While he was a wonderful worker and very good with the customers, his drinking escalated to the point where the customers noticed and reported him. Finally, he had to go. He had passed out in the back, and a customer found him.

One other employee really did me in. He was a nice young man from a nearby town. He lived in an area populated with a particularly large religious community. He worked really hard, always showed up, and had a great attitude. Then one morning I came to work, and the front door was open. I thought maybe one of the other employees had come in early, but the store was empty. I was really upset as that meant the store had been wide-open overnight.

I looked around and didn't see anything alarming, such as a riding lawn mower missing or anything like that. Unfortunately, when I went to the front counter to turn on the cash register, it was open, and there was no money inside. I stood there stunned and angry. Then it got worse. I looked down at the floor safe, and the top was off. All of the money in the safe was gone. The evening person always had the safe combination so they could put the evening sales in there at closing time. A little would be left in the cash register for the morning person to have change for the customers. It was all gone—every last penny. And so was the night guy, along with our company pickup. I called his parents and was told that he was an alcoholic. He periodically went off the wagon. In other words, he would just go get drunk for a few days or more. I told them about the money and the truck. They told me to pray for him. I didn't pray to God to help him. Instead, I prayed to God to give me my damn truck and money back. The truck was found several miles away, but I never saw my money again. My now ex-employee was found in Los Angeles, drunk on his ass. His religious community got him an airplane ticket, and he came back. A few days later, about fifty people from his church filled the parking lot. I went out to meet them, and they begged me to take him back. They said forgiveness was good for the soul. I told them that money would be better. Then I told them I was a Catholic. They all got in their cars and left. I never saw them or him again.

After several years, we had worked so hard, we kind of wanted to have normal jobs. We were working six and seven days a week. So it was goodbye to the hardware business. I sold the True Value Hardware Store, and it was off to another adventure. We invested all our money and decided to be like normal people. My wife finished her fifth year in college for her teaching credentials and taught fourth grade for the next twenty-five years. She later became a librarian and loved it. Me? Well, that story is a bit more complicated.

I had never worked for anyone else and had no idea what the hell I wanted to do. I went to an agency at the state of Oregon that helped people with career direction. After rigorous testing, it was determined that I "liked fixing things." Then they told me I had too much money and did not qualify for their job-training programs. So there I was, up a creek without a paddle. Actually, that old analogy is pretty dumb. I mean, if you are up a creek without a paddle, get out of the canoe, and walk out of the creek. Now up a river without a paddle is more realistic. Then you are really in trouble unless you are a good swimmer.

A few weeks later my neighbor Wayne asked me about it. I had always been super busy with work, and now suddenly, I was hanging around the house. Wayne owned a large steel fabrication company and needed someone to help run an industrial-supply store at one end of his business. For the next three years I worked in that store and loved it. We sold welding and other related supplies. We also took in welding and fabrication orders. The pace was incredibly fast, which suited me just fine. I also knew there was more out there and started going to night school at a local college. While I was in school, I had a couple more jobs as I was just trying to find myself career wise. I studied electrical and refrigeration. For three years I poured myself into this. It was part of the Building Trades Division of Portland Community College. It was in Northeast Portland and a long drive from Forest Grove. It didn't matter. I really knew the building trades were what I wanted. Three years later I had an electrical license and was licensed in refrigeration, also known as HVAC/R (heating, ventilation, air conditioning, and refrigeration). When my education was complete, I graduated and packed up my equipment. Before I could get out the door, the head of the Building Trades and Industry Department grabbed me. I was so enthusiastic through my schooling that he decided he would hire me as an instructor. I wanted to work in the field and not just be an instructor, so he hired me part-time. I fell in love with teaching and stayed there in the evenings for the next twenty years. During the day I had a few jobs as a maintenance manager. I would manage work crews in high-rise buildings in Downtown

Portland. The crew would do the light maintenance, and I did the electrical and HVAC/R work. I had finally found my place in the world of work. But a few years later I went to prison. Yep, you heard me right—prison.

Ron Goes to Prison

At the end of the first day in one of the Oregon Department of Corrections state prisons, I was waiting for my cell. About three thirty in the afternoon, I was told to go home and come back tomorrow. So at this point you are probably wanting some explanation of what the hell is going on. Sorry, I couldn't resist. I set you up. It's the Irish in me.

In the mid-1990s I was resting at home when the phone rang. A guy on the other end asked me if I wanted to go to prison. Before I could sound off with a round of f-bombs, I discovered he was a high school friend whom I had worked with a short while back. He was now working in a prison, and they were looking for a maintenance person with electrical and HVAC skills. I couldn't resist. Ron went to prison—except I got to go home at night. How cool was that? You are laughing, I hope? I was actually working on this book at the time, and I thought what a bunch of cool stories I could write about it.

Prison wasn't like the movies. It was actually okay. You came, did your work, and went home. I worked days and Monday through Friday. The pay was pretty good, and the benefits were great. However, keeping your distance could be challenging. A lot of them were really sad and depressed. It was hard not to feel sorry for them and get yourself in trouble for getting too friendly with them. Working in a prison as a guard can be really hard; the maintenance employees had it pretty good. The guards worked rotating shifts and days. They had to work on all holidays. They also had to discipline the inmates on a regular basis, leaving the inmates disliking them. On the other hand, the inmates liked us as we worked Monday through Friday on day shift and had holidays off. Working in the maintenance shop was a premier job. The inmates got to fix things and were trusted to walk around with tools. They stayed out of trouble for the most part as they did not want to lose their jobs in the maintenance shop. I worked at the prisons for a few years until I had to retire because of medical conditions related to Agent Orange exposure.

CHAPTER 7

SICKNESS

At about the age of forty I was in very good condition. I rode motor-cycles, hiked, ran marathons, and climbed mountains. I was incredibly healthy. But after a doctor's visit, I was told that my endocrine system was acting up. I was also told that I had diabetes. No one in my family had any of this, so it was a mystery to myself and my doctor.

Over the next twenty years I just fell apart piece by piece. I had so many medical problems, it was hard to figure out what was going on and how to fix it. I went from a hundred and sixty pounds to two hundred and fifty over about five years. Carrying extra ninety pounds made life difficult. I was on so many prescriptions, it was hard to keep track of them. I went from a man in perfect health to one in a cane, a walker, and finally, a scooter. During that period, I had more than twelve surgeries. For several years I was on pain medication. While they made life tolerable, narcotics were like dragging a fifty-pound rock around all day. I was sluggish and no fun to be around. Freckles' funny Irish humor was gone. It was just plain dead. To understand how I tolerated this for two decades, found the source, and recovered my health is a story all by itself. I returned to being the vibrant hiker, runner, and mountain climber once again. I went from almost dying to being an energetic, athletic, and happy grandfather. Today I am the luckiest guy in the world.

You might be asking yourself, "What the hell happened?" The answer came with an incredible discovery fifty years in the past. In a small military base in Korea near the DMZ in 1967, over five thousand miles from my home, something happened that would change my life forever. A dirty little secret lay dormant for all those decades. Uncovering the truth nearly killed me, but it saved my life and helped a lot of other veterans regain their health. Sadly, too many of them died without ever knowing what killed them. Many families lost their fathers, sons, friends, or husbands to a dark secret that was kept buried for nearly five decades. After years of investigation I discovered that chemicals had been sprayed at my base that caused many of my health problems.

In 1985, Dr. Timothy Gray Sr. in Forest Grove, Oregon, made a disturbing discovery. I had diabetes and problems with my endocrine system. From 1985 to around 2015 I had several broken bones as my osteoporosis worsened. I had lost bone density for decades. It was easy for me to bump into something and fracture a bone. One fall in a church ended in a broken femur. I had surgery to remove kidney stones at least twice. The bone loss caused small fragments to get stuck in my kidney, making urination extremely painful. The worse the bone loss got, the harder it was to walk. Here was this marathon runner and mountain climber bent over on a walker, dragging a dying carcass around the house like a bag of wet cement. In grocery stores, malls, and other big buildings, I dragged a three-piece scooter out of an old Volvo station wagon, put it together, and went about my way. The medical professionals were all confused. No one had an answer why. After years of X-rays, scans, MRIs, and tests after tests, they all just said the same thing, "We don't know why this is happening." One doctor said that all he could do was make me comfortable. Then he handed me a prescription for pain pills and left the room. I never saw him again.

On a Friday evening in late winter of 2009, I was feeling pretty good and agreed to help a young man do some electrical work at the Catholic church I attended. The work was not difficult or even physically challenging. Unfortunately, though, I had an accident and fell onto the hard marble steps alongside the altar. The maintenance worker was supposed to be my spotter. That job meant chasing tools, holding the ladder, and being there if the electrician fell or had any other problems. Then without saying a word that night, he just left. Maybe he was going home for dinner. I didn't really know why. He was gone.

Because of the bone-density loss, I severed my right femur. The first reaction to accidents like that often produced a laugh. I had seen people fall or hurt themselves in other ways, and their first reaction was to laugh. Suddenly, their mood changed as did mine that day. The second after I went down, I looked up and saw Jesus hanging on the cross. The sight of it made me laugh. To the best of my memory I said, "There you are hanging on the cross, and here I am at your feet with a broken leg."

Immediately after that the laugh subsided, and I felt more pain than I had ever known. I did not know that a human could feel that much pain and not die. I screamed my spotter's name so loud, you could have heard it all the way from the Vatican in Italy. There was no response. After about half an hour of yelling and crying, there was one sliver of hope. Off in the distance I could hear a priest and the church secretary closing up the office. It was Friday night about 5:00 p.m. Their voices carried softly down a long hall, through the area the priest put on his vestments (robes) prior to each church service. Even though my voice was beginning to go hoarse, I gave it all I could. Sadly, my cries for help were drowned out by ceilings thirty or forty feet high. The only things that heard me were the pews, walls, and an altar with Jesus behind it. I heard the big front door to the office and school slam shut as they left without even knowing I was there. I was alone now, thinking I would die there.

What had actually happened in my fall was, I bounced down those hard stairs and was flung under the front pew. There were no kneelers in the front pew, so I was just stuffed under there and could not move the lower half of my body. Next to my chest was a leg that should not have been there. The skin was still attached; however, the bone was completely severed. The leg was in two pieces. Any movement caused enough pain to make me nearly pass out. At one point I was able to free my arms and reach under the second pew to grab a daily missal as well as a songbook. I tried with all my might to toss the books through a stained-glass window and draw enough attention to get help. They just fell down and hit the floor before even touching a window.

Meanwhile my wife was getting worried sick as for nearly fifty years I had rarely missed a dinner meal. A sit-down dinner was mandatory in our household. My wife is German, and family dinners are important. Even though our kids are long gone, the two of us are there promptly at 6:30 p.m., eating dinner together, without fail every night of the week. That night I wasn't there. For over two hours I came in and out of consciousness, screaming loudly, begging God to help me. There was no way I would live through the night in that church.

"What the hell are you doing? Is this some kind of joke? Get out from under there!"

The voice was familiar, but I was still screaming from the pain. Then I saw him.

"I fell, goddamn you! Where the hell have you been? I fell. I'm hurt. I broke my leg after a fall. You were supposed to be my spotter. I have been lying here screaming for two hours. Call 911."

The maintenance man had gone home for dinner and had forgotten to put some tools away, so he came back. There was going to be a funeral the next morning, and he did not want the presiding priest to have to deal with the mess he had left. So he came back to clean up. Had he forgotten all about me? He kept on asking questions until I told him to look at my leg. That was all it took. He dialed 911. When the ambulance drivers looked at me, one of them quickly pulled out a needle. The only thing I felt was the syringe, and I prayed to God for relief. I screamed most of the way to the hospital. I was flipping around like a fish out of water inside that ambulance. The pain was so severe that nothing seemed to stop it. The EMT in the back with me tried as hard as he could to keep me still. I was just flopping all over, trying to get a comfortable position. Finally, I saw a second syringe come out, and a few seconds later I was out. Thank you, God. I woke up a day later in a hospital with Lydia at my side.

I was mad at God about it and did not set one foot in that damned church for five years. Eventually, some devout members finally helped me with forgiveness, and I came back. That was in 2014, and I have been going there ever since. For the life of me, I will never know why that guy just walked away without saying a word to me. I was mad at him for years, then finally let it go. Maybe he had said something, and I just didn't hear it. Maybe he thought I was going home for dinner myself and decided to do the same. Or maybe the poor guy just had a lot of things on his mind. I tried to find him one time later for some closure, but a church member told me he was no longer there.

In the spring of 2011, I had a parathyroid removed. I was told it was blocking the flow of calcium and vitamin D into my system, which was causing osteoporosis and bone loss. My thyroid was also failing, and I have to take a medication for that for the rest of my life. Medical professionals were really confused about all this. Not long after this, I was standing in front of a toilet at home, urinating. All of a sudden, I felt a huge push inside me, and blood came pouring out all over the toilet, the wall, and the floor. I was severely shocked and, for whatever reason, felt I did not have time to call 911. I firmly believed that by the time the police came, the fire truck arrived, and an ambulance was summoned, I would be dead. I am not a medical doctor. I just felt this to be true. I leaped into my car and tore out of the driveway. After about a mile into the five-mile trip to the VA hospital, clots prevented the blood from coming out, causing extreme pain. The blood started backing up into my system. I was bleeding to death internally.

Trying to explain what happened next is very difficult. If you are faint of heart, you might want to skip over the next few paragraphs. I knew I was not going to make it to the hospital unless I could do something fast. I just didn't know what that was. Cars were driving by, but no one noticed what was happening. I was praying to God for help. Suddenly, I realized I had a toolbox in the back of the car. I crawled over and opened the back of the car. I don't know if it was the voice of God or the desperation of a dying man. Without any more thought, I reached into my toolbox and grabbed a needle-nosed pliers (I am going to choose my words carefully at this point). I removed the clots. I pushed the pliers inside, grabbing a big glob of blood clots, and yanked. Blood came pouring out again, and the pain was relieved. Now I was bleeding both externally and internally. Although I had to stop two more times on the way to the hospital, the roadside procedure was working. Each time the flow of blood was stopped, I used the pliers to clear the clotting again. Although I was still alive, I was afraid I might run out of blood.

By the time I got to the VA, the inside of the car had blood all over in the front. I was covered in blood from my chest to my feet. I stepped out of the car, and that was the last thing I saw. The lights went out. Several veterans carried me to the Emergency Room, and I woke up there. Medical professionals were all around me. They were confused and started asking questions. As I was losing a lot of blood, they were pumping saline into my veins. Every few minutes they would tell me that the bleeding was stopped. Medical staff would start packing up and preparing to go to the next person in the ER, but within thirty seconds the pain would start again as the blood clotted in my penis one more time and was backing up into my body again. While the blood stopped coming out where urine would normally be draining, the bleeding inside me was still flowing. It took a brief moment for ER doctors to understand it was a continuously recurring problem about once a minute. A surgeon was called, and he went to work immediately.

The source of the blood were a couple of veins that had burst. Just a few weeks earlier I had a procedure on my prostate. Men over fifty often have problems with the prostate. Sometimes we have trouble urinating, sometimes there is cancer, or the patient may have both going on at the same time. After talking to a surgeon, I made a decision to have a transurethral resectioning of the prostate, also known as a TURP. The surgeons go in and shave the prostate down as it has been pressing against the ureter, causing pain and urination difficulties. If a man is in advanced ages, they may choose a TURP in lieu of having chemo, radiation, or serious measures. While a TURP does not cure prostate cancer, it can relieve its symptoms. For example, a ninety-five-year-old man may not survive chemotherapy and/ or radiation and choose a TURP instead.

After my TURP, there were some complications, and that was why a few weeks later the bleeding started in our downstairs bathroom that night. I spent a few days in the hospital to stop the bleeding, and then I was sent home. It was December 24, and our son and daughter-in-law arrived from New York City to spend the holidays with us. However, I told the doctor I was so afraid, I did not want to leave the hospital. I was so frightened that I still did not believe I was going to live. The doctors assured me I was going to be fine, and Lydia wanted me home with the kids for Christmas, so I gave in and went home.

I would like to tell you that all went well, but it did not. A couple of hours after Christmas dinner, it happened again. I should have stayed in the hospital. This time my wife drove me straight to the VA hospital. Before we left the house, I knew I had to face the clotting issues again. This time I simply used hot water. In the garage, I had the hot water tank set at 160 degrees. I filled a large pot with the water and jumped into the car. When the clots began to form, I just simply melted them by putting that part of my body in the water. It really hurt, but it kept the blood from clotting and causing the awful pain. It worked until I got to the hospital, which was all I needed. However, once we got there, the struggle continued. Things did not go well. As the surgeons could not get the bleeding to stop, I called for my wife. She was in the waiting room, and I needed her with me. I really thought it was over this time.

Lydia was brought into the operating room. There were so many medical people around me, working furiously, that she could hardly see me. I caught an occasional glimpse of her as I was barely conscious. Instead of needing about thirty minutes to stop the bleeding as they did last time, this time it took about three hours. At one point Lydia couldn't take it anymore and left the room. I cannot imagine what was going on in her mind. She must have been really scared. We had been married a long time. At one point, I gave up. I was in so much pain for so many hours, I just could not take any more. I told the medical staff that I couldn't take it anymore. I was done. Suddenly, I found myself in a dark tunnel. It was just like the ones you heard about when people died and came back. For the record, I never believed a bit of that nonsense. I just thought it was for religious ministers and Catholic priests trying to scare people into believing about God and the afterlife. And there I was, in that tunnel. I saw everything that other people who had this experience talked about. I was completely serene. I had no pain—not even the feeling we might have on the bottoms of our feet, walking across the kitchen floor. You feel your arms hanging from your shoulder. You feel your knees, thighs, and feet as you navigate to the refrigerator and so forth. I had no feeling whatsoever. I was just floating toward a bright light. I thought briefly of my family and then said to myself, "They will be fine. They will be here soon." I was just so happy.

My utopia suddenly faded away. I felt something pushing on my chest, and it hurt. Then a voice yelled out, "Breathe! Breathe!"

I woke up mad. I wanted to go back there and told the medical staff just that. They were too busy trying to save my life to pay any attention to my whining. Although I was angry, that dissipated soon. I had just been exhausted and tired of the pain. Today I am very glad I lived through that. A few days later, after the bleeding was completely stopped, I went home. Adam and Kelly had left as their vacation ended. I felt sad for them too as they were very worried about me. It must have been hard on them to see me go through something so traumatic, especially right in the middle of a Christmas holiday when people were supposed to be happy. Years later I would find out what happened in Korea that caused so many of my medical problems. Until then I just spent my days and nights struggling with health issues and numerous medical problems requiring surgeries. The cause of my problems would stay sealed for the time being.

In the fall of 2013, I started having blood in my stools. After months of this I had a surgery to fix the problem. I was tested for cancer as the VA doctors were suspicious about this bleeding. There was no cancer.

From about 2012–2018 I went to the VA hospital annually, every spring, for breathing difficulties. We often thought it was just due to pollen and allergies. We didn't know there was something more behind all this. We just didn't know what. For about thirty years I had been on puffers to help me breathe, along with rescue breathers for difficult times. In the spring when it got so bad, I would be given a nebulizer treatment, among other things, to help clear out my bronchial tubes and lungs. I had many different procedures, X-rays, scans, MRIs, and tests to understand why a healthy, active person was having so much trouble breathing. I was a nonsmoker, and I did not drink. Around 2015, I was told that I had several nodules inside my lungs, and it was not a good thing. I was asked if I wanted to go to classes to understand what nodules were and what kind of treatments would help. I accepted. I was tested for cancer again, and the diagnosis was negative again. I was relieved, but worried about the future.

At one point I went into the VA ER for a nebulizer treatment, and I was also having severe acid reflux. The treatment for this was just a GI cocktail as it was called. It was a mixture of something that did the trick really fast. The following day I was back again. They took some X-rays, and I waited in a room. Suddenly, the door opened, and there was a throng of people outside it. I was told to get up on a gurney immediately. I was reeled into an operating room as they saw something. Hours later, I woke up all groggy and confused. What they had found was a gallbladder situation. When the surgeon went in, he saw pieces of my gallbladder scattered around. Some of it was mush, some was hard as a rock, and the rest was in between. I was informed after the surgery that it looked like the gallbladder had blown apart maybe as long as a year ago. Maybe it was a slow disintegration. Regardless, he was very concerned that I had never felt it or the pain of infection. I had no idea of any of this. He cleaned everything out, and I was fine. However, a short procedure ended up much longer because of the condition of what was left of the gallbladder and how long it had been in that condition. After a few days in ICU, I was told the following day I could go home, but the head of cardiology needed to see me first. When older patients had difficult surgeries, they needed to be double-checked before going home. When she came into my room in ICU, she said that she was concerned about something. She said that often in older patients a heart might do a hiccup in the days following. She mentioned something about A-fib, a condition that had an irregularly rapid heart rate that might cause poor blood flow. That particular night she was walking around with another woman who was head of cardiology at a joining hospital, OHSU. The two of them talked to me for a few minutes, and suddenly, they moved in really close and were raising their voices. One asked me what was wrong, and the other wanted to know if I was okay. I laughed out loud. I was fine. Or so I thought. As professionals in the field, they noticed symptoms they were familiar with—something I knew nothing about.

Suddenly, their faces blurred, and I went out. I hit the floor. When I woke up, I was in a bed in a dirty workshop in the basement. Two aliens with huge heads were working on me. I tried to move and asked them what the hell was going on. They told me to hold very still and not to talk. I went in and out for several hours and finally woke up in a regular room. I told them about what I saw, and they started laughing at me. Apparently, I was on some good drugs to regulate my heart and do other things. I asked them if I could take some of those pills home. They told me, "no." The following day I went home.

Sometime around 2010, people in the VA hospital kept asking me when I was in Vietnam. Others would ask me where I was stationed in Vietnam. I had no idea what they were talking about. I told them that I was in Korea, not Vietnam. I had never been anywhere near Vietnam. Why were they asking me that? Then they would say, "Oh" and walk away. One night at home in the early 2000s, I was watching something on Vietnam and an herbicide called Agent Orange. It was a nasty herbicide that had been used to kill foliage so the North Vietnamese soldiers could not hide and do surprise attacks on US infantry soldiers. But along with saving lives by clearing out the jungle, the chemical was killing Vietnam veterans by the thousands. Veterans would come home from Vietnam, and years later, medical problems would start making them sick, and many died.

Sitting there listening to the documentary, I suddenly got scared—I mean, really scared. The narrator on this show was listing some of the conditions including internal problems, lung diseases, heart diseases, diabetes, cancers, neuropathies, and numerous other medical problems. One by one I went down this long list, and I had several of them. I just sat there with this hard knot in my stomach. I went upstairs to my computer and confirmed what was on that documentary. Then I went to Google and typed in something that would change my life forever, "Agent Orange in Korea."

At first, all that came up were Vietnam, Vietnam, and Vietnam. After a few hours of searching, I typed in something like, "I am dying of Agent Orange-related medical conditions, but I was in Korea." Computers were slower in those days. Finally, something came back. It had a woman's name and mentioned the possibility of Agent Orange (AO) in Korea. I clicked on it and saw a bunch of data. It was really confusing. I left a message and waited. A few days later I got a response from a woman named Tara King. She was thrilled to hear from me. She told me there was a small group of around six or eight people across the country who were in Korea in the late 1960s and had symptoms that mirrored what were making Vietnam veterans sick. I joined the group immediately.

For the next twelve-plus years I often spent around eight to ten hours a day on this project. I got up daily about 4:00–5:00 a.m. and worked all day—sometimes all night. I almost lost my mind. I was just utterly possessed with it. I was also mired in anger. I had gone to the VA, and they laughed me out the door again and again. I wrote letters to the VA in Portland, Oregon, and Washington, DC. I made hundreds of phone calls over all those years. The sicker I got, the madder I got. I filed claims for twelve years. Rejections kept coming. I was told that I was a liar, fishing for something that wasn't there. I was also told that I was a thief stealing the VA's time when they could have been helping deserving Vietnam veterans. A high-ranking official, who would remain nameless, told me that I was a disgrace to the uniform. I went home and cried.

Over the years, some of the people in our group died off from diseases related to the exposure to Agent Orange. Some just gave up after so many denials. We looked like a bunch of fools trying to find gold in the middle of the ocean. The saving grace was that we knew we were right, and that was what kept us going in the beginning. Ten years later, I was going at it alone. I stopped hearing from everyone except Tara and one man whose name I can't remember. Then I met an Air Force veteran who was managing a county office that helped veterans with their claims. I went there and met Doug. He was in Korea about the same time I was there. As he was farther south while in Korea, he was never exposed to AO. But he was really curious about this crazy guy (me) who was trying unsuccessfully to take on the VA alone, and why did he spend so many thousands of hours on this failing fishing expedition? Doug decided to take my case. I was thrilled. My family doctor joined in too.

Doug and my doctor worked together with me for years. Finally, Doug retired, and my doctor had done all he could. I was alone again, and the rejections kept coming in. Then suddenly, Doug decided to continue helping me after his retirement. I was ecstatic. Then I was referred to a woman working for the VA. For reasons of privacy I will call her Susan. Her job was difficult because of all the claims being processed. Adding another person, especially someone who was not in Vietnam, would be monumental. I was the first veteran in Oregon to file an Agent Orange-exposure claim who was in Korea. Susan and Doug had worked together a lot over the years, and I believe she took my case because of that. Over a few years she really started working hard, and I wasn't sure why, but I really appreciated what she did. Wherever you are, Susan, thank you.

One day, a long time earlier, I got an e-mail from Tara. She had a name of a man who was in Korea when I was there and had actually sprayed AO around my base, Camp Casey. Tara had got his name from someone who went to a veterans' rally of some kind. One of the speakers was this particular man. He told a small group that he had sprayed Agent Orange in Korea and was sorry for what he did. He knew that what he did sickened many Korea veterans and caused some of them to die. He felt terrible about it all. The guys at the rally reminded him that he was just following orders, and he shouldn't beat himself up so bad. Brush had to be killed off so we could see if the North Korean soldiers tried to break into the camp. We were guarding atomic bombs, and keeping them locked up was paramount. After the rally, he moved into the woods somewhere in

Washington and just wanted to isolate. He felt so bad for what he had done that he just disappeared. Attempts by me to contact the family failed. I had lost the only possible link that could have truly helped my case. I was devastated.

A couple of years went by, and one of the oddest things that ever happened in my life brought my case alive again. I was at a BBQ, talking with friends. The subjects of Vietnam and Agent Orange popped up. I told my friends about what I had gone through in Korea and how disappointed I was that I could not get the evidence I wanted. A man named Ed came up to me and said that his wife knew someone who had what she thought were pictures of someone spraying Agent Orange in Korea. I could not believe my ears. How could this be? Then I started worrying as I wondered if she could find this guy and if he would still have the pictures from fifty years ago. All I could do were just pray and wait. A week later Ed called me. His wife had the pictures.

There are occasional newspaper articles about someone who wins millions of dollars in a lottery and how excited they are as well as what they are going to do with all that money. That was how I felt that day. What was the likelihood of something like that happening? I thank God every single day for that miracle.

"Where Did You Get These Pictures?"

The man at the VA offices in Downtown Portland said just that when I came in with pictures that showed an American soldier and some South Korean Army soldiers spraying Agent Orange in different locations around Camp Casey. The man at the VA was just plain stunned. I knew what his next move would be, so I did something else before I came in. I figured he would deny my claim based on the so-called evidence being nothing more than pictures that could have been doctored to look like something they weren't. In other words, he would say the pictures were fake. If he did that, I had a backup plan. Another miracle had happened. I was contacted by the mother of the man in Washington who did the spraying at Camp Casey. He had agreed to sign a notarized document regarding his spraying the Agent Orange. The man's mother then mailed it directly to me.

Standing there listening to this upset VA employee was very interesting. He was scared because bringing something like this into the VA offices was opening a real can of worms. There would be levels upon levels of high-ranking officials arguing and trying to figure out how to get out of this. Years went by, and the rejections kept coming although I knew it was only a matter of time. Every time I got another medical condition that was related to Agent Orange, I would file a new claim. Soon it would be denied. They hoped I would just give up as many vets did. They just got too sick to fight anymore. However, I would not give up. I had lost a good career and had to retire on social security disability at the age of fifty. I was as sick as a dying dog a lot of those years, and fighting for my VA benefits was my primary cause. I swear, there were times it kept me alive. Besides, with the evidence I had given them, the VA now knew that I was telling the truth and that I had the evidence to prove it. Sooner or later, they had to give in. Then it happened. It really happened. After a decade and a half of hard work, I won. All those years of driving my wife crazy, all those years of research and struggling—they just ended.

Some people think I was mad at the people at the VA. That is not true. Although one that I mentioned upset me, I knew that they did not know. All those people who were denying my claims truly believed that I was a nutjob as Agent Orange was never sprayed in Korea. They held on to that until the bitter end as levels after levels of management never knew about AO in Korea. No one knew until I presented absolutely true documentation and photos. Did someone know? Sure, there might have been a few, but they were either long retired, dead, or working somewhere across the country, and none of them knew anything about Ron Weber from Portland, Oregon, filing a claim. No one connected the dots.

On a dark, rainy day, I walked down to the mailbox as I had done a thousand times over many years. It was Friday. The big manila envelopes from the VA, carrying another denial, always came on Fridays. I used to get excited and tear the envelopes open right there at the mailbox. After years and years of denials, I was not excited or anxious when I opened the mailbox. There sat another big manila envelope with another denial. I didn't even open it. Back at the house I just tossed it on the dining room table and went about my business. Later that evening. I took the envelope up to my office and decided to get the bad news over with. I sat down and opened it.

"Service connection for diabetes mellitus associated with herbicide exposure is granted."

I panicked for a second and started reading page after page explaining the decision. It was not a denial. It was an acceptance. I had won a claim based on my diabetes, which meant the United States Veterans Administration out of Washington, DC, had approved a claim that accepted the fact that Agent Orange was sprayed in Korea in the late 1960s. I contacted Susan on Monday, and it was true. Another employee at the VA told me that I was the first veteran in Oregon and probably nationwide to win a claim like this. It was a huge decision on the part of the VA to admit that this herbicide was actually sprayed in a country other than Vietnam. My story made the front page of the *Oregonian* newspaper, the largest paper in the state.

That Friday night I wept. I just cried and cried. Twelve years of hard work finally bore the fruit I needed. My deep thanks to Dr. Gray, Doug, Susan, the man (and his family) who sprayed this herbicide in Korea, Tara, and the others in our early support group. I also want to thank so many other who helped put me over the top, not to mention the extremely odd happening at Ed's BBQ, where the deciding evidence was discovered as well as my dogged research and refusal to quit. I was so relieved, I was beside myself. I knew there was a lot more work to do as I was only service connected for diabetes, and I had a lot of other medical issues that I believed were a result of my exposure to Agent Orange. I had won a big battle, but I still had a lot of fighting ahead for myself and thousands of other Korean veterans across the nation. Over a few more years I won claims on tinnitus, peripheral neuropathy on the feet and hands, lung disease, and PTSD. Looking back on everything, I had one other odd happening. On the Tuesday before I discovered I had won, I got down on my knees and prayed. I had adopted a bunch of African and African

American grandchildren. I wanted to help them and put money in a college fund. The problem was, I did not have enough money for this big dream of mine. I prayed devoutly that Tuesday night, asking for God's help, and said that "if I win this claim, I will use the money for the kids." Three days later I won. Is there a god up there pulling all the strings? Is there an afterlife waiting for us? I don't know and probably never will on this earth. I just pray to a Creator and leave the rest to whatever happens. I give thanks for my life, my wife, our two sons, a wonderful daughter-in-law, the grandkids, and all the wonderful things that I have received in this life, especially the odd and unexpected things.

The Recovery

Another unexpected happening was the reversal of my health. Once the VA accepted my exposure to Agent Orange, they started fixing me. About nine years ago, I parked the scooter and started going all over with a walker. I bought one of those with the big rubber tires and walked with it all over the neighborhood twice a day or more. Soon I was walking pretty fast. The neighbors thought I was going nuts as after a few months I was running up and down the street with the walker. Then I started trail running with the walker. The looks and comments I got were either criticism, confusions, or praise. I kept this up for about a year and started building muscle. I also started swimming at the local 24 Hour Fitness.

What started all this recovery were a lot of things. Primarily, when my parathyroid was removed and the thyroid treated with levothyroxine, my endocrine system began working again. This helped with the pain. The next step was a lot trickier. Since medical providers had pretty much given up on me, I too was hopeless. My only friend some days was the narcotics for pain. As I started to improve, so did the pain. I also started feeling better mentally. I was beginning to feel hope for the first time in years. Confidence that had disappeared from my life started showing up too. As I knew the pain medication helped me, I also knew it was dragging me down. I decided it was time to start letting go of it, as my body was healing and I didn't need the pain medication as much as I did before. I reduced my OxyContin dosages by five to ten milligrams a month. It was a slow titration downward. As this drug was long-lasting, I also needed something that was fast acting for difficult short-term pain. That was Percocet. The reduction plan was really difficult as I had been on these prescriptions for a long time. However, by the end of one full year, I had gone completely off the OxyContin. I went down slowly to keep from problems that could occur when people went off a prescription too quickly. Next was the Percocet. I decided to do the same thing. I set up another twelve-month plan, going down slowly. At the end of two years, I was off everything. That was over ten years ago, and I have never taken a single pain pill again. If I would ever have a broken bone or invasive surgery in the future and seriously needed pain relief, I would use them as prescribed and get off them as soon as possible.

During the time I was going off the pain medications, I continued exercising. I finally got off the walker. By the end of the pain medications, I had also put the cane aside. Walking without any aids was so exhilarating that I could hardly describe it. I was ecstatic. I had been lying around in bed and using all these aids to walk for so long that I could only dream of the hiking, running, and mountain climbing in my past. But now my body was coming alive again, Slowly, I began hiking. Then I bought a pair of Nike running shoes. I could not run on pavement and still don't do that. So I started running on pine needle-covered trails in the forest. The pine needles made a soft carpet, and the shoes made it even easier. I would only run for short distances at first. I went on a healthy diet too. During all those sick years, I was eating comfort food, which helped me get up to two hundred and fifty pounds. I could only dream of being thin again. The scale in the bathroom was now hiding behind some shoes in the closet.

A few months into the slow return of my health, I dragged the evil scale out of the closet and weighed myself. I was two hundred and thirty-eight. I had lost twelve pounds. Three months later I was two hundred and twenty-five. With the endocrine system working, the narcotics gone, the walking aids gone, and a good diet, I really started feeling hope. I was so excited that I kind of went overboard. I became a regular at 24 Hour Fitness and kept on hiking. Two years later I was done to one eighty, then one seventy, and finally, about three years later, I was back to one hundred and sixty pounds. At almost seventy-two years old, I don't run much anymore. I hike and ride bicycles. I am completely back to where I was decades ago. What a crazy ride it has been.

The best part of the whole thing was mountain climbing. From the age of twenty-one, when I got out of the Army, to about fifty years old, I had climbed Mount Hood in Oregon about twenty-five times. It is eleven thousand two hundred and fifty feet tall. While I didn't summit all those times, I fully enjoyed it. Sometimes I would get shut out by the weather and had to turn back. There were also days when I just was too tired. The cold, the wind, and the heavy snow just were too much. It could be as dangerous as hell. If it got like that, I just did the smart thing and turned back. At the top when you were going up something called Hogsback, people died every year. Either a lack of skill or the right equipment or other factors would be the cause. My best days there were taking up my two sons with me. What a blast. Those were days I would never forget.

I also climbed Mount Saint Helens before and after it exploded as well as many mountains in the Northwest. Now those were all in the past. Or so I thought. Around 2014, I got this hairbrained idea to just give it one more shot—one for the Gipper. I had this training program I had used for decades. On January 1, almost every year for decades, I would start the training. It entailed walking, hiking, running, and workouts at the gym. One of the primary exercises was walking stairs. I used this as climbing mountains could be similar to going up stairs. In Downtown Portland, there was a building that was forty-two floors up and three floors down, for a total of forty-five flights. I would walk or run this building once a week from January to May. Then I would make the climb. My only climbing times of Hood were from May 15 to June 15. Any other time frame often was a disaster. Too early and you got stuck in snowstorms. Too late and you got into really slippery wet conditions, or you fought the rocks.

Every year, someone got injured or killed from slipping on rocks or being hit by falling rocks.

When I reported to the forty-five-floor building in 2014, it had been about ten or fifteen years since I had been there. In a few of my early sick years, I insisted in crawling up Mount Hood. It was foolish; however, it gave me a sense of accomplishment. In 2014 I was really nervous. I was sixty-five or sixty-six years old and was recovering from a decades-old series of bad health. I started in January, and everything on me hurt. Arthritis had really set in over those sick years. By May I was sort of ready. What we always did in the past was to leave Portland at 10:00 p.m. Two hours later, at midnight, we were boots on the ground on Mount Hood. This timing was important as we enjoyed watching the sun rise from on top. You had a three-hundred-and-sixty-degree view. Sitting there, eating lunch, and watching the sun show itself were memories that I would never forget. I was alone a lot over the years as I couldn't find any of my friends who could do it. They said they wanted to. However, when they saw the training program, they backed out. It took a lot of discipline to climb mountains, and it was just too much for a lot of people. What I did were just find climbers on the mountain and join them.

May 20 came, and at midnight I had my headlamp on with spare batteries and my breathing puffers in my pocket, along with an electronic locator in case I needed help. On my back were food, drink, and a first-aid kit. I took the first step, and excitement just took over. Off I went. But things didn't go as I had hoped. Clouds set in, and visibility sucked. At 5:00 a.m., I was not on top as I had planned. I was so sore and slow that it would take me three hours more to get to the top. When I got to Hogsback, it seemed steeper than I remembered. The trick to getting up was taking it slow and easy. As you reached the top of Hogsback, it narrowed. To the left if you slipped, you were gone. You would drop down a longways and would likely die. In the middle, there was always this nasty crevasse. Sometimes it was ten feet wide, and sometimes it was twenty. If you fell in there, you probably wouldn't be found until the snow melted in the summer. To the right was a slippery slope that ended you up in Devil's Kitchen. A long slide would land you into the sulfur pits.

If you didn't die from the fall, the smell of the sulfur would finish you off. I crawled my way up, and at the very top, there was almost zero visibility. Although I was thrilled that I made it one more time, I was disappointed about the view. It took about forty-five minutes to get down off Hogsback while the rest of the trek down was relatively easy. I had done it again. I was so happy, I cried. This broken-down old goat waiting to die had recovered completely. I left that mountain to never come back. I had proven my point that I still had it, and I quit while I could. There was no way I would die up there. I would find a different hobby.

In 2015, I did it again. Then I went up in 2016, 2017, and 2018. I also climbed Mount Adams three years in a row from 2015 to 2017. It was a thousand feet taller than Mount Hood; however, it was not technical like Hood was. Adams was just a shitty long haul, with a stunning view at the top. My friends thought I had lost my mind with all this climbing. They were probably right. I am not sure what my wife thinks as she rarely talks about it. However, she does get mad sometimes because I always tell her that "I'm only going up a little way this time." Then I would call her from the top. I do that so she won't worry about me. Then she calls me a liar, and we have a good laugh. Even though she worries a lot, she knows how much I love to climb. On September 13, 2018, I turned seventy years old. I wanted to do something cool for my birthday. I wanted to summit one more time. When I got up to the lodge, it was closed as it was midnight. Outside the lower lodge was a sign-in desk. I signed in, letting them know that someone was on the mountain. As it was off-season, I was alone. I had never climbed Mount Hood off season. It was a bit risky, but I wanted to climb it on my birthday. I had all the right stuff, and off I went. It was once again really slow as I had a knee replaced a year early, and I had the usual arthritis issues for someone my age. As the summer had melted a lot of the snow, I spent a great deal of time on the rocks. That part really sucked. Eventually, I made it up. Even though it was cloudy, it didn't really bother me. I had been up there several times on sunny days. I was just glad that a seventy-year-old ex-cripple could do what I had just done. About halfway down, it started to snow heavily. I was surprised as it was mid-September. I was completely alone. There was not a single person to be found up there besides myself. I wasn't worried, though, as I had my locator and cell phone. I sat down a minute for a sandwich and a drink. I reached into my pocket to get my phone out. I liked calling people on the way down and bragging. When I tried to make a call, I discovered the battery was dead. Later I would find out that I had just tossed the phone in the backpack, and a water bottle or something had bounced around, turning on the phone, and a video ran in the dark of my pack until the battery died—bad luck for me. No problem, I had my locator. I searched around, and it was nowhere to be found. When I got back, the locator was sitting on the passenger seat of my car. Oops. I started moving really quickly, and in about two hours, I had gotten below the clouds and snow. Around noon I still had a couple of hours to go. I was really sore and was moving a bit slow. Around this time the winds were whipping really hard, and I thought I heard a human voice. That happened sometimes when I was in a thick forest. The whipping winds made howling sounds and other noises as they bounced off trees. But that day I kept hearing something that sounded like a human voice. Finally, I saw something moving in the fog off in the distance. I moved toward it, and about five minutes later, I saw two young men. They were dressed in shirts, light pants, and tennis shoes. When they reached me, they wanted to know if I knew the way down. They had decided to take a little hike up there and got lost. I told them that I had never been up there before and wasn't too sure myself how to get down. I watched their faces droop and then told the truth. I thought my little Irish joke about being lost up there too was funny, but they didn't. I guess I really scared the crap out of them. But that is what they got for going up there unprepared. Had I not stumbled across them, their bodies might still be up there. In the summer of 2020, I did it again just before my seventy-second birthday. I went all the way to the top. I hadn't planned on doing that, but the sun was out and visibility was perfect. But it was also difficult as my age, arthritis, the new knee, and a few other things made it hard to climb. I should probably quit, but sometimes it is hard to give up on things you love so much.

CHAPTER 8

DESSERT

After a fine meal comes the dessert—usually something sweet and tasty. The following are some more great stories that I was unsure of where to put in the main body of my book. So here is your dessert.

1.   The Buick Roadmaster

In 1970 I had a Buick Roadmaster. It was a 454 without a single smog device—over four hundred horsepower just waiting to hit the road. I was drunk coming out of a bar in Portland one night, and a state patrol car caught me doing about 80 mph just west of the city. I did not see him. He was just sitting there in the westbound ramp right where the Sylvan Grocery Store used to be. I saw some flashing lights in my rearview mirror, and down the ramp he came. By now I was about a mile ahead of him. I was totally pissed—another fucking ticket and probably a DUI as I was drunk as a skunk. This was not the first time the cops had chased me along this particular stretch of road. I started to slow down and face the music.

Suddenly, I took my foot off the brake and put it on the gas pedal—hard. If I was going down, it would be in a blaze of glory. Quickly, I was going about a hundred miles an hour. The officer must have been confused with my car slowing down and then speeding up. At 2:00 a.m. on a Saturday night / Sunday morning, this cop probably figured I was drunk, and he was coming hard at me. When we got to about a hundred and twenty miles per hour, I noticed that he was not gaining on me anymore. Then it hit me. He was driving a new test vehicle that the Oregon state police were using on a pilot program to save money on vehicle costs and gas. They were driving these two-door, six-cylinder tiny Mustangs. Ford Motor Company had gone away from the cool-looking muscle cars to this economical smaller version. This Mustang was topped out.

I nailed it to the floor. The Buick was a Roadmaster station wagon, so the long roof to the back, combined with the heavy weight of the car, was keeping the wheels on the ground. Just before the Hillsboro Airport cutoff, I saw red-and-blue lights flashing on a parked car. It was another state cop with the same kind of car. The officer might have been radioed by the first officer. He was out of the vehicle, probably waving at me to pull over. I went by him at around a hundred forty miles per hour. He was just a blur. The road was a four-lane highway that was straight and perfectly flat for about twenty miles. It was a great place to see how fast your car could go.

I looked in the rearview mirror and saw the red-and-blue lights fade quickly. He probably did not even bother getting in the car to start it up and come after me. The first car was also nowhere in sight. They knew they could not catch me. I think they probably also thought the chase could have ended up in a fatality and backed off.

I will never forget how good it felt. I mean, I still can feel the adrenaline pumping.

Speaking of nut balls on the road, I was one of those too. Drinking while driving was one of my favorite hobbies for a long time. I don't know why I never got in a bad wreck nor got a DUI. I could have killed someone out there. I guess I was just really lucky.

One of my worst stories was with my wife and two small children in the car. Someone behind me that night was flashing his lights for me to pull over. I couldn't. The road was too narrow. He was trying to pass me on this windy road. He got so close to my bumper, I thought he was going to hit me. At one point I just slammed on my brakes. I was ready for war. He slammed on his brakes to avoid rear-ending me. He was pissed and went flying by me on a corner. I got really mad and started tailgating him. By this time, I was out of control. My wife started yelling at me, but it did no good. He had scratched the rear quarter of my car when he passed me. Finally, on a straightaway, I pulled around him and smacked into his driver's door. We were swerving back and forth, trying to have a destruction derby. While my wife was really upset, I think our two little kids thought it was fun. Ironically, we were both driving those tiny, early Hondas. While it was dangerous and stupid, some of the other cars on the road were really enjoying a live and moving Honda destruction derby. They didn't even have to pay an entrance fee to see two comical maniacs going at it. Finally, one of the two of us quit. Probably, it was me as the other guy didn't have a wife and two little kids in the car. When we got home, I went straight to bed and passed out. *Go, Ron.*

2.   How to Make Money

When I was ten years old, a neighbor of ours by the name of Ray Fountain decided I should mow his lawn. I was this skinny, little kid with a mop of red hair and ten thousand freckles scattered unevenly across a pale, white face. I was so Irish white that if I took my shirt off, I would look like a sheet of typing paper with two white broomsticks under my torso that I walked on. My face looked like a Norman Rockwell painting gone bad. I would have made a great scarecrow. Thank the good Lord, we didn't have a garden at home as my mother would probably have planted me out there to keep the scarecrows away. Needless to say, I was not Superman.

So there I was, looking straight at the handle of this gigantic mowing machine that looked like something between Godzilla and Frankenstein. I didn't want to do it and hoped he was just fooling around with me at my young age. Then Old Man Fountain, as we called him, said he'd pay me a buck. That might not sound like much today, but in 1958 any kid with a buck was rich. I started fantasizing what I would do with my newfound wealth. I thought about the box of Cheerios and the Nabisco Premium crackers. I would put peanut butter on them and eat a whole ream at a time. And I didn't forget the Oreo cookies. I would get some of them too. In my mind that buck was gone before the blade on the lawn mower spun around once. I couldn't wait to get that beautiful green buck. It would be the first dollar I had earned in my whole ten years. I was a businessman now. But there was a roadblock. I had to face the monster parked in front of me. That monster was a Briggs & Stratton three-horsepower motor on top of a tin can with four wheels and a handle. Painted on the side was, "Montgomery Ward's Lawn Mower."

The old man was tall and well-built with a constant mean look on his face. He always had a beer in one hand and a cigar in the other.

"Go ahead, kid. Start it up."

I had seen my big brothers mow our lawn with one of those push mowers. There was no motor on it as we had a small, flat lawn. Mr. Fountain's mower was different. I stood there looking at a chunk of black rubber attached to a white rope on Ray's gas-powered mower. Next to that I saw a small sign that said, "Pull." After nearly peeing on myself out of fear, I grabbed the rubber and pulled. It didn't move. A voice behind me said, "Harder."

I gave it all I had, and the rope came out a bit. The blade started to turn. I was on my way. Then my hand slipped off the rubber, and I fell down on the tall, green grass that needed mowing.

"Both hands."

I grabbed on with both hands and used all forty-seven pounds of me. This time I would defeat the monster. If Superman could do it, so could I. But Superman wasn't there that day. I got the blade to move around a bit more with the biggest pull I could muster up. Nothing happened. It didn't start. I looked up at that mean face and was pushed away.

"Get out of the way. I'll start it, and then you push it. I want every blade of grass cut before you get your buck."

When Ray pulled the cord on that machine and the engine came alive, I nearly ran home. It was so loud that I put my hands over my ears. The cheap metal body of the mower shook like a penguin at the North Pole in the worst of winters. Mr. Fountain kept motioning for me to push the damned thing. When I didn't respond, he opened his wallet, pulled out a dollar, waved it at me, and made a motion for me to push the angry big monster. While fear had me in its deadlock,

I found a spark of greed inside me that drooled over the green buck staring me in the face. I took my hands from my ears and was off with a big push—sort of. At least I was able to make it move. The yard was huge. This was going to be really hard.

Old Man Fountain followed me all over that yard, drinking beer and smoking that cigar while laughing as I struggled. It was like he was walking on a horse track, following a newborn stallion, and egging it on to see how far it could walk before falling on its face. Unlike the yearling I would not fall down. I wanted my money. Maybe I could save it and buy some beer and a cigar when I grew up. Instead, I blew it and spent the money on junk food. Now I would have to mow Ray's lawn again the following week. Surely, I would save the dollar next time. It didn't happen. The snacks at the nearby grocery were calling my name. Every week I made a solemn promise to save the money. I never did.

At the age of ten, I loved the idea of earning money. So I started delivering newspapers for the *Oregonian*, a morning paper. By the time I was twelve I was mowing lawns, delivering papers, and babysitting. I had it worked out so that the paper route was in the morning, lawn mowing was after school, and babysitting was at night on the weekends. I was the richest kid on the block. I really liked the idea of working for money. However, I never saved a dime. I loved junk food too much, and I was so skinny that my mom thought I had a tapeworm in my stomach, eating my food. I would eat and eat and eat, but I could not gain weight. Dad was gone now too, so it was okay for me to spend my money on cookies, crackers, and candy bars. If he had still been at home, he would have given me the belt and taken the junk food for himself.

In high school I kept doing those three different jobs and added a part-time job at a Dairy Queen hamburger joint. I would close the place at night during the week. Now I had four jobs: papers in the morning, lawn mowing after school and daytime on weekends, after-dinner cleanup at the Dairy Queen during the week, and babysitting on weekend nights. The only way I could do homework was at school. I would make sure I had my homework done for the first class in the morning. Then during that class, I would do the homework for the second class. The trick was to look up a lot and give good eye contact. Nod, smile, and do anything to let the teacher think you were paying attention. Next, look down at your homework for the next class and write a sentence or two. I made it look like I was writing down what the teacher was saying when I was really doing homework for the next class. Then in the second period I would be doing the homework for the third class and so on. I did that for four years and never got caught. Talk about a guy who had attention deficit and was hyperactive. Wow. I was off the map. Today, in my seventies, I am still that way. I just used it for productivity. While a lot of kids took medication for it, I just overworked, and later became a husband, father, worker, coach, writer, and about anything else I could do, often at the same time. In the end I still have ADHD. I love it because I use it to accomplish things, help others, have fun, and do lots of other good stuff.

After serving my country, while I was going to a local community college, I had to once again face the lawn-mower brigade because I needed money. Besides, lawn mowers had improved in the three years I was gone. They had better mufflers and were easier to start. Some were even self-propelled. The good news was that the eager rich people nearby were glad to have an Army veteran mowing their lawn. It was back to work now. I went to college in the mornings, had an afternoon job delivering the *Oregon Journal* newspaper, mowed lawns before and after the midday newspaper route, and worked in a parking lot in the evenings. I worked as a cashier in a booth at the parking lot, which gave me time to do homework between paying customers. I also did homework while in class, just like I did in high school. Hurray for ADHD. Somehow, I got good grades too. This time I saved my money as I wanted to start a business. As I hadn't really robbed Meier & Franks, I would have to learn how to save money on my own. After several years, I started a motorcycle shop and finished college with a bachelor of science in business management. I was also married by this time.

Still, I wasn't done figuring out ways to make an extra buck or two. I decided to open a small engine repair in the back of the hardware store. I saw a sign on a competitor's building that said, "We service what we sell." As soon as I did the same, I started selling a lot more lawn and garden equipment. Customers liked being able to buy something and have the person who sold it being able to fix the equipment if it broke down. Besides, I worked nights and weekends repairing all kinds of small engine equipment, and it increased my income. During slow times, the extra money really came in handy, especially after we had our second child.

Years later we wanted to take our two sons to Disneyland. But money was tight. Lydia taught at a local grade school. I had a day job and still repaired equipment in the evenings for years after we sold the hardware store. Coming home from work one day, I saw a bunch of workers striking. They were striking over wages and benefits. When I drove by, I could see the signs they were holding up. I also saw a big sign on the front of the building. It said they were hiring temporary employees so they could keep the doors open while they negotiated with their permanent workers. I worked there for about a month on swing shift, stocking the shelves as the delivery trucks arrived. A month later, the strike was ended. They got a raise in pay and benefits too. I was happy the strike was over. Working two jobs was really hard, and I didn't like being a strikebreaker. We used the extra money I earned to help us go to Disneyland. We had a great time.

Another way for me to earn extra money was fixing things. I finally got my electrical license and my heating and air-conditioning credentials. I could do plumbing too. So anytime I wanted to buy a new welder or any other equipment, I just did some work on the side. Another great source of income was part-time teaching. After I finished my schooling at a local college in the Trades and Industries Department, I was asked to stay and teach. I did that for twenty years in the evenings. Beyond that, I am still trying to figure out how I can earn more money. Maybe this book will sell. What can I say? I love earning money. The best part of making it is that I get to spend it having fun with my grandkids.

3. The Riot

In the spring of 1992, I was visiting my brother Rick in Los Angeles. When I got there, I was told that there was a riot about forty-five minutes away. Living all my life in quiet Oregon, I had never seen a riot except on the evening news. They were always somewhere else. So at the age of forty-four I decided to go check it out. Going to visit a riot was not a very intelligent decision to make, but my life in a small town an hour west of Portland, Oregon, was pretty boring. I was in Southern California. I was looking for excitement. I was also writing articles for an African American newspaper in Portland. I thought it might make a good story for the paper.

I borrowed a car from my nephew and drove north to the area where Rodney King was arrested and nearly beat to death by the police. This attack on King was what started the riot. The black community was tired of being harassed by the cops. And King's near-death was like lighting a keg of dry gunpowder. For a few days that part of Los Angeles looked like WWII.

When I pulled off the freeway, I followed what appeared to be low and dense circles of black smoke. Soon I seemed to be transformed into a distant war zone. Off to my right was a large building on fire, and behind me were several former homes that were now nothing other than smoldering ashes. Black men were running everywhere. Their frightened women and children huddled in fear wherever they could. Some of the men were running from car to car, bashing each one of them into oblivion. An angry large man quickly moved into sight. He was eyeballing my nephew's Toyota sedan. As our eyes met, he lunged straight at me with a tire iron raised above his head. I drove out of there as fast as I could, knowing if the car got trashed, I would be buying Ryan a new one.

I really had hoped just to see what was going on from a distance, not actually be in the middle of it. It was too late. There I was in the dead of one of America's worst riots in our country's history, and I had no idea of how to escape. Suddenly, I saw what appeared to be some police cars. Slowing down, I got hopeful as they would surely help me. The closer I got, the more police cars I saw. There were hundreds of them. It was as though every cop car in Southern California had joined up in this massive parking area that had room for about five hundred cars. The lot was full. As I started to come to a stop, about a dozen or so of the cars started flashing red-and-blue lights. A loudspeaker from the closest car warned me to leave the area immediately.

Not a single officer from any of the cars got out. They just sat in there staring at me with shotguns across their hip and shoulders. I guess they were all waiting for the command to go in and stop the riot. I kept thinking that maybe if I got out of the car, they would see that I was white, and maybe that would help. Then I thought better of it. I just slowly drove away. I think I was more afraid that day than most of my days in Korea. I did see a convenience store up ahead. The lights were on, and people were inside. I pulled in and walked to the door. I was immediately met with two or three shotguns and told to get the hell out of there. I got in my car and drove off.

The farther I drove, the closer I got to the violence. Along the way, people were throwing rocks and furniture through their own front windows. Finally, they would pour gasoline on the front steps, light it, and run to the middle of the street with the other neighbors, watching all their homes go up in smoke and flames. Some took what they had left, put it in their cars, and drove away. Others burned their cars too, then just sat down in the middle of the street and cried. Several blocks away, I saw a large mob to my right, in the middle of a parking lot. They were milling around, looking angry and bored. I heard a lot of yelling, and suddenly, they just turned on one another and fought with the only things they had left in the world, their bare fists. I had never seen anything like that before. It was like a black hole somewhere in the galaxy, turning itself inside out.

Suddenly, what appeared to be an angry mob engulfed the car. The driver's side door was ripped open as though it was never even bolted on. A hand grabbed my arm like a vise, and a loud voice screamed at me, wanting to know what the hell I was doing there. I tried to explain that I was with an African American newspaper from Oregon. I heard the voice again.

"Are you listening to me? What the hell are you doing here? Get the hell out of this place, you damn idiot."

I could hardly breathe. Gasping, I didn't know what to say or do. As the car door slammed shut, a large man in a National Guard uniform screamed out to his men, telling them to remove a road-block back to the same freeway I was on earlier. The only difference was that I would be going south instead of north. Finding a lone white guy driving around near thousands of angry blacks really surprised this guy. He wanted me out of there, where I belonged. As a group of angry-looking guardsmen glared at me, I drove up the ramp and was out of there. My head was spinning. I remained southbound for nearly an hour without muttering a sound. To this day I don't remember a thing about the drive back to my brother's house. It was like some surreal trance. Many years passed before I had the nerve to tell Rick about what I had done. Ryan, if you are still out there somewhere, I am sorry for almost dying and ruining your car.

When I got home to Oregon, I wrote an article titled, "Curiosity Almost Kills the Cat." The publisher liked it. My wife didn't. In the aftermath, it was determined that fifty people died, two thousand three hundred were injured, and over a thousand buildings were damaged or destroyed. The damage estimate was over a billion dollars. And I managed to make it out of there in one piece. Although my article got fifty bucks and great ratings, thirty years later I am still asking myself if it was worth nearly dying—not one of the smartest things I have ever done.

4.   Ron Weber—PI

The Case of Michael vs. Michele

So there I was, retired two weeks, and I was bored already. I was out taking a walk one morning, hoping to get hit by either a stray bullet or a fully loaded log truck. So far, retirement sucked. Then she appeared—the woman who might have just saved my life. Well, she didn't exactly appear. Rather, I saw her name on the backside of an old, rundown building. The sign was so small, it was hard to see, like she was not allowed to let anyone know her line of work. Actually, that was probably true, except for people who needed her help.

Beneath the sign was a basement door into what looked like an old and nondescript office building that had been closed for a few years. Had I not looked back at the hot yellow Corvette as I walked by, I would have never seen the sign. The door was solid with no windows and a doorknob that looked like someone had tried to break into the building a few times. Curious about the cool car, I slowly walked over to take a closer look. I would have preferred to move a bit quicker. There was no way. I had retired early with medical issues, and at the age of fifty I looked more like I was near eighty.

Standing in front of the car, I felt a bit of warm air. When I touched the hood, it also was warm. I looked around to see where the driver of the car would be. All I saw was this crappy-looking old building. Maybe a successful real-estate agent was inside, trying to figure out how to rent the small place. Boredom and curiosity got me again. I walked toward the building. At the door, I assumed it would be locked. To my surprise, the door opened up. I had to go in.

Once inside the building, I saw a woman's name and logo on a small door to the left. A sign on the interior door showed the same name as the one outside above the front door. I assumed that it was an old sign from a prior business in this apparently empty building. When I opened the door, I was expecting to see a broom, some mops, and a bucket or two. However, it was not a janitor's closet after all. It actually was a tidy small office with a woman sitting there working on a computer. I still had my hand on the open door and looked back at the little sign on the door again.

LINDA JOHNSON P.I.

There sat a woman who was a real live private investigator.

She seemed like a nice person; however, as you spoke to her, you could tell she was very good at finding people who did not want to be found. Thusly, she herself didn't always want to be found. She was in the exact line of work that she should have been in.

"Can I help you with something?"

I wasn't sure what to say, so I just opened up my mouth and said the first thing that came to mind.

"I recently retired from the Oregon Department of Corrections and am looking for something to do. Do you have any part-time work? At this point I might even volunteer some time."

Linda also did not mince words and stopped me dead in my tracks when she heard the word *volunteer*. I felt I was done for and needed to run for the door before she tracked me down and made me promise to never show my face in that old building again. Our eyes briefly met, and I thought maybe she would see something good in me. At least I hoped she did.

"Why would you want to volunteer for a PI? Were you a corrections officer?"

I didn't want to tell her that I was actually a maintenance electrician and HVAC mechanic although I had to. I explained that some medical problems had made it unsafe for me to work in the prisons, and I had to retire early. I was not ready to retire. I was desperate to find some kind of work that I could do. I had already secured a part-time teaching position in a local college and was just interested in trying a few different things. Then my mouth made a nose dive.

"I am a great driver and have a nose like a bloodhound. If you need someone to do some surveillance work, I would do a great job of that."

Actually, I was full of shit. I had no idea of what it took to be a private detective. But I had read an article in *Reader's Digest* about thirty years earlier on a PI. I was ready. Linda was not buying it. Then I threw the curveball. It was my Hail Mary pass—the only one I had left.

"I am also a volunteer for a local police department."

I did not bother to tell her that I had only been a volunteer for about two weeks. It didn't matter. At this point, I was somewhere between Magnum PI and a piece of garbage. I wanted to be a productive member of society, and things weren't looking too good in that department. *Come on, Linda, help me out.* As it turned out, she did. Although she probably just felt sorry for me, it didn't matter. A few days later, I was with her partner on a stakeout. I was in heaven.

This case was not exactly something that would make the big-screen movies although it would give me an inside track to the life of a PI. However, after about fifteen minutes I realized that a lot of their job was just sitting in a car, hoping to see the person they were looking for—not as exciting as the old television show *Hawaii Five-0*, with the handsome Tom Selleck. My new partner sat across town, watching a different location, probably wondering why a guy my age would volunteer for something so boring. There I sat, for hour after hour, trying not to fall asleep. Finally, Linda radioed us back. The bad guy was not going to show up tonight.

So what was this big case? It was not exactly rocket science. A man named Michael and his wife, a Russian woman named Gertrude, owned a couple of foster homes that were care facilities for the elderly. The homes were about thirty miles apart, and they hardly ever saw each other. Basically, he lived in one house, and she lived in the other. They would get together for drinks and dinner about twice a week, and if he got lucky, they got in the same bed. That was that. She was not happy and suspected he was having an affair. In fact, she was dead certain he was with another woman named Michele and hired Linda to find the bitch.

The trouble with this case was that it required us to follow Michael, which turned out to be almost impossible. He worked inside this house for at least one eight-hour shift. Then he also slept there for another eight hours. In between, he had eight more hours in a day, and he spent that cooking, watching TV, reading, doing laundry, and so forth. After a few days of watching the place, we discovered that Michael rarely came outside. His only human contacts were a man whom he hired to work swing shift and a lady for graveyard. Their only tasks were keeping an eye on the three elderly people in the home. They were able to dress and bathe themselves. They only needed light supervision. As Michael worked day shift, he was free in the evening to do whatever he wanted to do. It seemed like he would work during the day, eat and watch TV or read books in the evening, and sleep the rest of the time. That seemed somewhat normal as he lived in the house. The two other workers did their eight hours and went to their own homes. We were pretty much helpless in finding Michele or whoever the woman was whom he was allegedly having the affair with. He apparently was not sneaking out to see her as the backyard had a six-foot-high fence, and we could see his driveway. His car just sat there. Also, no one was coming to the house to visit him. As far as Linda's partner was doing, he was driving around town, hoping that maybe Michael was scaling the fence or had another way out. The partner was hitting the bars and clubs, hoping to find Michael with his new lady. After several nights of this, I was really getting bored. Then it happened.

About 9:00 p.m. on a Saturday night the front door opened, and out he came. He got into a car and backed out of the driveway. The chase was on. I was thrilled. I followed Michael for about five miles and watched him pull into a parking lot. It appeared to be a bar or a restaurant. After a couple of minutes I mustered up enough courage to follow him in. I had no authority to even speak to him and had called Linda and her partner to let them know where Michael was. However, we did not want to lose him, so I went inside to see if he was meeting Michele and taking off in a different car with her. Then I would get to follow him in a different car. Or I would be the clown who let him get away. How exciting.

After seeing Michael at a table, I sat down nearby, but not close enough for him to be suspicious of me. So far nothing out of the ordinary was happening. Michael was sitting at the bar and chatting with another guy about the same age. Suddenly, I felt some hands on my shoulders, giving me a light massage. I turned to see the beautiful Hollywood starlet whose soft hands were now rubbing my lower back. It felt great. However, when I turned around, I was met by this good-looking guy, who asked me if I wanted a drink. I was really taken aback and felt like I wasn't much of a detective or private eye. There wasn't a woman in the place, and I hadn't noticed. It was a gay bar. I almost started laughing at the poor guy standing there in front of me. I was still sitting and kind of reeling from my inability to notice things. Working in the prisons, I was taught to always be aware of my surroundings, but I failed the test on this one.

I thanked the man and bought him a drink for the great back rub. Then I told him I already had a date for the evening. What I didn't tell him was that it was with an alleged wife-cheating scumbag. By then Michael and his friend were kissing. Then they got up and danced for a while. Soon after they were back at the table, kissing again. A bit later they hugged and went their separate ways. Michael left the bar, and I was on the chase again. I was then very disappointed to find out that he just drove back to the foster home. How boring. I wanted more action. At least, though, I had solved the case. Linda was thrilled. Her partner was embarrassed that I had discovered what was going on. I was hoping that Linda might find out who the guy was and where he lived so Michael's wife could go beat the crap out of him. In the end, we discovered that the other woman was not a Michele. The culprit was a Michael or something like that.

After it was all over, poor Linda had to tell the woman who had just paid her a couple of thousand dollars that there were good news and bad news. As I was leaving, I heard Linda on the phone say, "Well, Gertrude, there is no other woman. However…"

I did not stay long enough to hear the rest of the conversation. That was all Linda had for me, and I called her the following week to thank her. It was very nice of her to let me taste a bit of the life of a private investigator. While I never became a PI, I did volunteer for a local police department for twenty years.

5.   The Lost Dog

When the doorbell rang, I assumed it was a friend or Amazon dropping off a package. When I opened the door, a frantic woman started yelling at me.

"Where is my father's dog?"

A couple of weeks earlier a cute little male dog showed up in our backyard. I knocked on doors for several blocks in all directions, put up signs, and contacted the local animal shelter. No one knew whose dog it was, and no one had contacted the shelter, looking for him. I even took him to a large park nearby. I walked all over the park, and no one knew him. However, one family wanted him. A few more days went by, and I returned to the park. I was getting desperate as I was allergic to dogs with long hair.

After another trying attempt at the park, I gave up and started for home. Before I could leave, the family who wanted the dog showed up again. The couple had two small children. The mother begged me for the dog. She explained that they were from Vancouver, British Columbia, and were at the park for a huge softball competition. The mom said they had a large-fenced backyard, and the kids would take good care of him. While I was considering it, the two kids were playing and wrestling with him. They wanted the dog, and the dog wanted them. I simply left him with them and walked home. My sigh of relief was deep although it wouldn't last long.

"Where is my father's dog?" I heard again.

The woman pushed past me and walked into our house, searching for the dog and calling out to him. When she did not find him, she opened the sliding glass door to the backyard and went out calling for him. But he wasn't there. The woman was really getting hysterical. The woman lived down the street, but I did not know her. A year after the death of her mother, she took her dad on a vacation to Mexico. Her dad lived in an apartment complex and had no place to leave the dog while they were on vacation. His daughter had a large-fenced backyard, so they decided to leave him there. A friend of hers would stop by daily to feed and walk the dog. But the dog had other plans. He dug under the fence and escaped, showing up in my backyard. After returning from Mexico, they discovered the dog was gone. The father was heartbroken as the dog was a fiftieth anniversary gift to his now-deceased wife. It was all he had left of her. However, they soon were told by neighbors that I had the dog at my house.

"Where is my father's dog?"

I tried my best to explain the situation to her. But it was to no avail.

"Canada? Canada? Are you kidding me? My father's dog is in Canada? That dog is the only connection my father has with my mother. Mom died, and you give his dog to a family from Vancouver, BC? Dad will die if I tell him that. He bought her that dog for their fiftieth anniversary. You get our dog back now!"

The next day I called the parks department and found out what group rented the baseball field that week, and the race was on to find the pup. It turned out that the family actually lived a hundred miles north of Vancouver. We lived just outside Portland, Oregon. Needless to say, they were devastated when I called. After a few days they called me back and agreed to return the dog. The families met at the Canadian border, and the man got his dog back. As for the Canadian family, they bought a puppy for their kids, and all was well. As for me, I learned a few lessons. One was to be careful with stray dogs. Would I do it again? Probably. It's just the kind of guy I am.

6.   The BBQ

One day my wife was out of town for a couple of weeks, and I decided to throw a BBQ. We had this wonderful seven-burner unit that was really too big for just the two of us. Although it was bigger than we needed, Home Depot had a closeout sale, and I got it for a great price. There I was, with my grill that could have cooked all the burgers, hot dogs, and sausages for a small army. The day of the infamous BBQ arrived, and I had more than enough food. With a couple of dozen grandkids and a few of their parents, things could get a bit wild. Usually, it would be a broken glass or maybe some Sheetrock repair and paintwork after someone fell down the stairs and put a hole in the wall. Actually, on this day, I was getting some help moving a huge, old TV we had in our upstairs bonus room. With all the helpers, I figured we could get it downstairs just fine. Someone lost their grip, and a two-hundred-pound TV and cabinet slide down a couple of steps and hit the wall. It was a miracle it didn't go through the wall and out into the front yard. Good thing, two of the guys at the party were sheetrock workers. With the material and paint, I think I got out of that mess for about a hundred bucks. Lydia never noticed a thing. All these years I never told her. If you meet her on one of my book tours, please don't say anything to her about it.

My good friend and father of two of my grandkids, Andre, was and still is a great cook. We decided to have him be in charge of the cooking. We had enough people that day for all seven burners to be going. Andre was cooking up a storm when I heard my name being called out.

"Ron, the BBQ's on fire."

Not to worry, folks. I got it. I mean, Ron thought he was somewhere between Superman and the captain of the local fire department. I could handle it. I had a full glass of grape juice in my hand—we are talking at least twenty ounces. Without even a blink of the eye, I tossed the juice at the fire, and it appeared to have gone out. The word *fire* had gotten a lot of attention, and the witnesses were amazed at how quickly I handled the situation. All the guests, except for Andre, were thrilled. He had been wearing a nice light-colored shirt and pair of pants. Now they were stained from top to bottom with grape juice. As he was yelling at me about the shirt, I heard, "Ron, the BBQ is on fire again."

When I looked, I saw what looked like an eight-foot-long stainless-steel bomb totally inflamed with a five-gallon propane bottle just inches from the flames. When I had bought the BBQ, I remember reading something about not using water on a grease fire. I forgot all about that and ran for the garden hose. If I had just remembered to have a fire extinguisher nearby, the fire would have been out in about three seconds. Apparently, I had other plans. By the time the grease had burned out and the fire quit, half of the guests were soaked and pissed off. Water had been flying all over. More importantly, the propane bottle could have exploded and killed or burned several of us. To make things worse, Andre and I were so busy cooking and entertaining people, we had forgotten to empty the grease pan under the burners, and that was what started the fire in the first place. Oops.

My old Catholic mother used this old expression, "madder than a wet hen." I think Andre was now madder than a wet hen. I was hoping that by hosing him down along with the BBQ, the grape juice would be off his shirt—no luck. Now he was purple and wet. Also, the once rectangular BBQ was now a melted blob—eight hundred dollars down the drain. We were both really embarrassed.

Some of the guests were asking why the flames were so high and consistent. A small grease fire would have gone out fairly quickly.

Somebody then asked me if there was something else under the burners that could account for such a huge and hot blaze. Then it hit me. When I had first purchased that BBQ, some wooden-handled tools came with it. I had completely forgotten them as I rarely ever used them. All I needed was a metal spatula that hung above the BBQ in our gazebo. Besides, we only ever used a couple of burners, not all seven. The intense heat from all those burners ignited the wooden utensils I stuffed in a little drawer beside the burners so long ago. Now I needed to verify if the fuel for the fire were those utensils. With one big yank the warped drawer opened up and exposed four or five of these tools burned clean, down to the stainless-steel part of the handle itself. The wood was gone. They had been toasted for real.

After it was all over, there was still enough food left for the rest of the day and then some. So we decided to sit back, enjoy the day, and laugh it off. What a great story it would make later for Ron and his book. However, there was still one little piece of unfinished business that had to be dealt with. In a couple of days my wife would come home from her travels. She would be sitting in her usual spot, reading the paper in the kitchen, and surveying her beautiful backyard. The conversation might go something like this.

"The backyard looks great, honey. Thank you for watering everything while I was gone. It all looks… Wha—Uh…um… Honey, why is the BBQ covered? It's the middle of July. We never put the cover on until October or November."

"BBQ? Oh, that BBQ, uh, I dunno, I guess I just spaced out and covered it up."

"It looks weird. I mean, even with the cover on it, the BBQ looks odd, like it is warped or something."

"I'll check it out later. I got some stuff to do right now."

Oh god, Ron, you are so busted. Run for your life. As soon as Lydia opened the sliding glass door to the backyard, I knew I was screwed.

"What is that horrible smell? It smells like there was a fire back here."

In the end I could not do anything but laugh. When she pulled the cover off that blob of melted metal, her face looked like something from the television series *Grimm*. I don't remember exactly what she said. I just know it wasn't good. I also heard about it for a long time afterward. The whole thing still makes me shudder and laugh at the same time. It took me two days to cut the thing all up, using welding torches and steel-cutting tools. I hauled it all off to a scrap dealer and gave it to them for free. Then I went to Home Depot and bought a new BBQ. It was much smaller. Shortly after this, Lydia went on another trip. This time she went to Australia and New Zealand for three weeks. Andre, the party is at my house, but no grape juice and no fire, please.

7.   The Front Desk

Not long after I started teaching, I took a friend to a local police department. He had to pay a fine for driving without a license. He was going to drive down there to pay the fine, and I told him that was not a good idea as he might get arrested again. So off we went in my car. While he was standing in a long line to make a payment, I waited in the front entrance of the building. People were coming and going like bees in a hive. There was a tremendous amount of activity, and a lady sitting at a desk by the entrance was directing people where to go in this very large building.

When things slowed down for a minute, I struck up a conversation with her. I told her about the last few years of my work in the Oregon prisons. Before I knew it, I was handed an application to volunteer. I spent the next two decades sitting in that front desk on Fridays. It did not require hardly an ounce of physical labor beyond running my mouth. I soon learned where every single office or cubbyhole was in the three-floor large structure. Listening to complaints was also part of the job, especially driving citations. I must have heard hundreds, if not thousands, of people whining about those. Me too. It has been a lot of years since I got a ticket though I am certain I definitely whined about it to the judge. I am sure she just laughed and made me pay.

The city-hall building held the police, the mayor's office, and about two hundred hard workers. The police department had about a hundred officers. The city population was nearly one hundred thousand. Consequently, there were a lot going on. My shift was absolutely crazy because on Friday afternoons, the first floor was crammed with people paying their fines before the weekend. If they did not get this done before Friday afternoon, they could face higher fines or jail time. Friday was payday for a lot of workers, so they filed in to pay up.

Another really busy event on Friday afternoons were passports. On the second floor of city hall, the Passport Office was just around the corner from the elevators and across the hall from the stairs. There were a few chairs in the middle of a small hallway. To paint a scene of what it was like would take an angry Norman Rockwell on a really bad day or, possibly, an artist who had experiences with painting mobs and riots. The upstairs was normally packed on Fridays by around 2:00 p.m. By 3:00 p.m. there were about thirty people standing in a place that would normally hold about twelve bodies. I had to hold people downstairs in the main lobby after the upstairs was full. By 4:00 p.m. there were normally about seventy-five to a hundred people in the building, expecting to complete their passport-renewal paperwork that day. While a passport representative could process about one person every fifteen minutes, that meant only two more people were going to get their passports renewed. The other thirty upstairs and the dozens downstairs were going to go home empty-handed. Usually, an additional processor was added on Fridays though that would barely help. A lot of disappointed people still would leave very angry.

One possible solution would be to hire and train more passport processors except there was not any money in the city budget for that, and we never knew from week to week how many processors would be needed. If we had five processors and it was a slow day, they would be sitting at their desks, doing nothing. There was just no way of knowing, so we did the best we could.

There were always yelling and complaining. My job was to calm everyone down, which was often impossible. I explained that they should come earlier in the week and earlier in the day. Many parents would get off work early on Fridays. They would also take their children out of school early and bring the whole family in to renew their passports. They also wanted to make it a long weekend by leaving work early. This made it a nightmare. If things weren't bad enough, a lot of the people planned vacations and then showed up at the last minute. When they couldn't get processed, they would just explode. They were stuck with the possibility of losing airfare and hotel charges. The only thing we could do was send them about three hours and two hundred miles north to Seattle, Washington, where emergency passports could be purchased. When told this, people would blow up in our faces and run out the door. It was bad enough for the paid staff. Just imagine what it was like for volunteers. Some days a volunteer might want to quit and walk out the door over it. Oddly, I was good at it. After working in prisons, I was used to all the chaos and complaining.

In addition to the driving fines and passports, there were other difficult situations. One of them was sexual assault. The victims were usually women, and it was no easy task for them to drive to a police department, walk in the door to be greeted by a happy big smile from a chatty volunteer, and ask for a female officer. I saw this many times over two decades and knew right away what to do. I would sit them down in a semiprivate area in the front lobby, offer them something to drink or eat, and get a female officer. I cannot imagine how hard that had been for them. Fortunately, I was raised with the gift of compassion and did the best I could.

Another difficult situation was fraud. Weekly, I saw victims coming in the door, crying and frightened. Someone had tricked them into giving them a lot of money. They would plead with me to contact the perpetrator and get their money back. But there was nothing that we could do. The perp was probably thousands of miles away or across the ocean in some other part of the world. For that matter, they could have been across the street. There was no way of tracking them. It was also something that the officers did not even want to address. There was really nothing they could do to help as the money was gone, and whoever took it was nowhere to be found. Unless it was for an insurance claim or a major crime, there was no point in filing a complaint. And as a volunteer, I could only console them.

The one that sticks to me the most was a small third-world woman who came in crying and screaming. She had come to America ten years ago to find the American dream. She got a janitorial job and kept it for ten years. She had saved and scraped every penny she could. She had over ten thousand dollars in the bank that she was going to use to go to school so she could get a better job. Now, everything she had saved all those years was gone—every last penny. To make it worse, the guy was on her cell phone, demanding more money. She handed me the phone, and I took it. While I shouldn't have, I was so saddened for this poor woman, I just wanted to do something for her. I went outside the front door and unloaded on the guy. When he started yelling at me, I lost it. I told him I had a tracking device, and as I was ex-military, I was coming for him. I doubt he believed me. Finally, he got tired of my ranting and hung up. I gave the woman her phone back, and she left crying. I never saw her again.

While there were a lot of pain and sadness within a police department, there was goodness too. The police worked really hard to make the world a better place. Sadly, most people didn't see that. All of us volunteers reached out with kindness toward the officers. We always made an effort to brighten up their days. Over two decades I got to know many of them on a personal basis. They did a great job of making our town safe, and I never quit letting them know it.

One of my favorite things on the front desk was when deaf people came in the door. I was an avid signer and enjoyed communicating with them. Several used to come in on Friday afternoons just to chat with me. The police took note of it, and soon I was being called in when a deaf person was either in trouble or needed help. A lot of times there were domestic situations. That was very common as when deaf people were upset, it was not like two people just raising their voices. Rather, there were arms flying all over, and sometimes if they were upset, they would make frightening guttural sounds. Maybe a deaf couple were just having a heated conversation that would never end up in abuse or physical fighting, but a hearing person wouldn't know that. Often onlookers would panic and call the police.

With the Americans with Disabilities Act of 1990, deaf people gained a lot of ground. They were given the right to have a licensed interpreter present when they needed one. It would take a lot of time and effort to make that happen. Major changes didn't happen overnight. They would have to slowly work through the system. I still socialized with my deaf friends. If we were ordering at a hamburger joint, I signed to them, asking what they wanted, and they would sign back to me. Then I just told the waiter or counter person. If one of them wanted to go look at used cars, I went with them and interpreted for them. When it got to hospitals, courts, and other serious situations, they were allowed to have licensed interpreters. In the past, deaf and hard-of-hearing people were stuck with anyone who knew even the smallest about sign language or pen and paper, which took a long time.

The first steps of the ADA for the deaf took years as there were hardly any licensed interpreters around in 1990. With the passing of the ADA, the local community colleges were suddenly facing crammed classes in a program that took at least two years. It was also not an easy program. The courses were designed for the deaf and known as American Sign Language (ASL). What I had learned was called Signed English, which was more of a rudimentary form of signing. The more formal language and most commonly used by the deaf was and still is ASL. They would tolerate Signed English although they preferred ASL as it was faster and clearer for them. A perfect example was for a hearing person who spoke English to try listening to a foreigner who spoke poor English and did so very slowly. As signing was just a hobby for me, I supported the ADA one hundred percent. With it, life for the deaf and hard of hearing got a whole lot better. It also improved for me as by just trying to help both the police and the deaf person, I often got in some tough situations.

As licensed ASL interpreters could now get a more reasonable wage, schools were flooded with applications. Because of the lengthy time it took for a student to be competent, it would be several years later before there was a large enough pool of interpreters to handle the demand. As time passed, the ADA was able to open up more doors for the deaf and hard of hearing. Most large businesses who hired deaf workers were now required to bring in licensed interpreters for interviews or other necessary communications, such as disciplinary actions. One example might be a good friend of mine (a deaf woman) who worked in a clothing store in Shipping and Receiving. Her job was to help unload the trucks, install price tags, and stock shelves. Her employer was struggling with her regarding issues like how to handle seasonal goods or special holiday sales and understand when old stock needed to be moved into special sale racks to move the merchandise quicker. On a few occasions I was asked to come in and meet with the manager and my friend. Overtime, problems continued, and she almost got fired. Finally, I told the manager about the ADA and said we needed to bring in a professionally trained and licensed ASL interpreter. She balked as it was costly. However, I explained that if she did not do that, she would be breaking the law, and my friend had a legal right to sue the company. The interpreter was able to explain the problems in more detail. My friend finally understood all that was expected from her by the company. Twenty years later, she is still there and enjoys her job.

Sometimes, though, the line was crossed on emergencies. Before the passing of the ADA, I tried to fill in until a licensed interpreter could be found. One example was when I got a call on a weekend night. I was told that a small, deaf girl had been kidnapped by an angry grandmother. The parents were moving to California that weekend. They had four kids, and Grandma decided that one of them should stay with her as she didn't want to be alone. She was a hearing person, but signed enough for the family to understand her. The deaf parents were at a police department, going out of their mind. The grandmother had left a note with them while they were in the backyard and informed them that they would be fine with just three of the kids and that she had taken one for herself. I was located and went to the police department immediately. At first the parents demanded a licensed interpreter. As it was a Friday night, none could be found. After a lot of haggling, they agreed to use me for the moment. We drove in police cars, looking all over for the grandmother. Hours later, she was discovered about twenty miles away. She had been picked up by the police in a small town east of where we had been looking. She agreed to bring the child to a county sheriff's office near where we were. She came and was detained by police officials. The child was returned, and the family left. They didn't even thank me. I think they were too upset about all that had gone on that night. Hours later a licensed interpreter contacted the police, but it was all over by then. Sometimes we just had to do the best we could.

Somewhere between 2005 and 2010, things started to even out. The deaf and hard of hearing were getting more of the representation they needed. Then something else began to change. With the advent of smartphones, iPads, smart televisions, Zoom, and many other electronic advances, interpreters are not needed as much as they were. As for me, arthritis has set in a bit, and it is hard for me to sign these days. Time just moves on.

There is one event at that police department that I will never forget. I had finished my shift and was getting ready to go home. The front doors had automatically locked as they always did at precisely 5:00 p.m. Since the police department was open twenty-four hours a day, there was a buzzer outside for anyone who needed to either get in or talk to an officer. As I was locking the front desk, the buzzer went viral. I went to the door, and a man was yelling. I refused entry as he seemed out of control. I told him we were closed, and I would call an officer for him. He was so angry, he nearly broke through the glass. He looked high on something. I went to the bathroom, and when I came back, he was in the building, shouting and running all over. One of the staff had let him in through an electronic devise from an inside office. I quickly exited through a side door. As I got to my car and opened the driver's door, I saw three officers enter the lobby. I remember mumbling something to myself about how we should have never let him in. However, I do believe that the police were just trying to help the poor guy. They were just doing their job.

I did not hear the gunshot. I had gotten in the car and turned on the radio before the weapon was discharged. When I got home about thirty minutes later, the news was on, and my wife was staring at it. Right after I left, the man ran straight at three officers and knocked them all down. He then grabbed one of their guns and fired it. By the grace of God, no one was hurt. The officers got control of the situation, and he was arrested. Apparently, he had overdosed on mushrooms or some similar drugs and actually came to the police department, seeking help. Suddenly, the hallucinogens took over, and he lunged at the cops without warning.

In 1775, the first weapon fired at the beginning of the American Revolutionary War was called the shot heard around the world. Although the shooting at that police department that night might not have been heard around the world, it was surely heard all over America. But I came back the next week. How could I not with that kind of excitement? About two or three years later, I retired from my volunteer job at the police department after twenty years. It was just time to do something else.

8.   I Want to be Atheist

Looking back at my Catholic upbringing, I am amazed at how hard the religion was put in front of us. I remember going to early-morning church five days a week before school classes and then again on Sundays. We also had daily religion classes as part of our school curriculum. That was just the way it was in those days. During WWII, churches in America filled up as families prayed their loved ones would make it home. After winning the war, most American families flocked to church in relief and celebration. Now that I am a bit closer to the end of my life than the beginning, I think a lot about those days.

One day on the front desk at the police department, things were a bit slow. Even people reporting crimes were not coming in. Usually, we got a lot of that. This day was unusually quiet for some reason. A man came in and asked to talk to an officer. I let the duty officer know, and he said an officer would be out shortly. The man had some questions about trespassing. He was with a local Mormon church, and kids were hanging out in the church parking lot on weekend night. We talked briefly about religion, and then the officer came. The Mormon man—whose name, I believe, was Paul—came back a little while later after talking to the officer. He had no other business there that day, but seemed like he just needed someone to talk with. He stood by the front desk for a long time. We just chatted about this and that. I told him that I was Catholic and then surprised him when I pulled out the *Book of Mormon*. The look on his face was quite amusing.

He asked me why a Catholic would be reading the *Book of Mormon*. I told him I was studying the competition. That brought a smile to his face. I explained that in my library at home, I had several versions of the Christian Bible, the *Torah*, the *Koran*, books on Buddhism, Confucianism, and Taoism, and other similar books. I just liked reading them. I enjoyed different views on God and religion. We chatted for about two hours, and I got some great information from him about his Mormon religion. Then I dropped a bomb on him by telling him that I wanted to be an atheist. The look on his face was a bit puzzling.

Little did he know that I was setting him up for some good old-fashioned Irish humor. We Irish are that way. We drop a bomb and then leave the room. My mother taught me how to do this. She would have friends over for drinks, cigarettes, and anything else the Irish liked to consume. With a room full of women at a party, she would sip a little whiskey, take a long puff of her stinky menthol cigarette, and then say something like, "So, Margaret, how long has your husband, John, been playing around with his secretary?"

Then she would quickly leave the room with a big grin on her face and bright-red lipstick smeared around the corners of her mouth. She got that stuff all over the end of her white cigarettes too. Thanks, Mom, for teaching me how to drop conversational bombs.

So I went on to tell Paul that we Christians had it tough. I mean, we were expected to believe so much that it sometimes seemed almost too much. You see, many religions throughout the world believed that Abraham, Jesus, Mohammad, and others were prophets. However, we Christians believed that Jesus was the son of God who came from a virgin woman who wasn't even married. If she was a virgin and a single woman, how the hell (sorry, Jesus) did she get pregnant? Sister Valerie Ann used to smack my fingers with a wooden ruler whenever

I asked her that. She told me that God took care of these matters, and we were just supposed to have faith. We were to believe what the Bible said and not question anything we didn't understand. We were taught that God sent the Holy Spirit to make Mary pregnant. At the age of nine I was still trying to figure out who this Holy Spirit guy was and why we called him that. Shouldn't he have a name like Bob Smith or something like that? Then my parish priest told me that we couldn't see Mr. Spirit because he was invisible. Telling a kid seventy years ago that a ghost got a virgin pregnant because God told him to was a real stretch. Then when we were told that Mary delivered the son of God, we asked the sisters if we could go outside and play. They said no. We had to finish our religion class first. Next, they told us that this Jesus guy could heal the sick and bring people back from the dead. What's a poor third grader supposed to do with that? I was too busy being a kid to deal with it. Then when they told us that Jesus died on the cross, went to hell, came back alive again, and ascended into heaven, I reached into my backpack and took out one of my many *Superman* comic books. Maybe God was where Superman got his powers. I would have to think about that for a while.

In the third grade I told our parish priest, Fr. Schaefer, that I had some questions regarding the Catholic rosary, which we were required to say continually. The Hail Mary has a part in it that says, "Holy Mary, mother of God..." Now wait a minute. First, she was a virgin that must have done something with this Holy Spirit guy to get pregnant. Then her son was supposed to be the son of God. That would make her the mother of the son of God. But the rosary told us she was the mother of God too. So did that make her the grandmother of the son of God? I didn't know Jesus had a grandmother. Did you? I was confused. I better knock it off now, or I will get in trouble with God. I already got in trouble with Fr. Schaefer for asking all those questions.

The nuns were only issued wooden rulers. Priests got these long wooden paddles. He used it on me that day. Ouch! Regarding all the questions I used to ask him, he told me, "Knock it off." That was a well-used saying in those days. Another one was, "Cut it out." Then Fr. Schaefer told me to have faith, worship God, and just believe what the Bible told us. He told me that when I was an adult, I would understand a lot more about Mary and her role in the life of God and Jesus. Fr. Schaefer told me it would all make sense when I was grown up. I wasn't sure about all that, but I decided to worship that wooden paddle that day and stop asking questions. Decades later, I still went to St. Anthony's twice a week for mass. These days, with the coronavirus-19, I watch mass on my computer. I also say the rosary every morning as soon as I wake up. I was a very bad little boy and needed a lot of forgiving. I told Paul that day at the police department it would all be a whole lot easier to just be an atheist, and we wouldn't have to worry about all that stuff. We both had a good laugh, and Paul went on his way. I wonder if he thinks I am an atheist now.

9.   Downing the Duck

Do you remember the county fairs and how much fun they could be? One of my favorites, besides the rides, was often called downing the duck. You had these little rifles with corks or something similar. You aimed, pulled the trigger, and if you were lucky, you would hit the moving duck and knock it into the water. You won a prize. When I grew up and went to work in the prisons, downing the duck had an entirely different meaning.

One morning, after I had been working there for only a few weeks, I had a hard job for one of the inmates to do. I picked someone, and he moaned about it. After morning break, he noticed me sitting at my desk with a poppy-seed muffin. He begged me for it, and I told him no. I did, however, promise him, if he got the whole job done in one day, I would give him one. He did just that, and the following morning, he got his muffin. I had one for him and one for me. Then he went to work on me. He really started in on me about how hard he worked the day before, and he wanted both of the muffins. Like a fool, I gave him both.

A few hours later, my boss came in, screaming at me.

"You gave an inmate a narcotic pain pill? What the hell were you thinking?"

179

I was fired on the spot. However, I protested and told him that I did nothing of the kind. I was informed that during the inmate lunchtime, this particular inmate went to the medical unit and said he was sick. He told a nurse that he begged me for a pain pill and that I had given him one. The nurse took a blood draw, and it tested positive. When I told them about the poppy-seed muffins, they knew what had happened. In those days testing methods were not as sophisticated as they are now. If you ate a couple of those muffins, the poppy seeds would cause the test to be positive for narcotics or something else in your system that you shouldn't have.

That was downing the duck, also defined as getting a prison employee in trouble. I kept my job, but I never gave an inmate anything to eat again. As far as that inmate was concerned, I fired him from the maintenance department and sent him to wash dishes. Had I gotten fired, this inmate would have gotten a lot of kudos from all his buddies. I was a hell of a lot more careful about any contact with inmates after that.

10. The Woman Officer and the Chewing Gum

I hope the military today is not as tough as it was fifty-five years ago. It seemed like we were always getting in trouble for even breathing. On my third day of Basic Training, I overslept. My sergeant came in and woke me up.

"I see you overslept, Weber. Why don't you just sleep some more, and when you feel like getting up, come out and join us."

I thought that was really nice of him and got up about an hour later. When I walked out, I saw all the other basic trainees doing calisthenics. The exercises looked really hard. Finally, the sergeant saw me.

"Well...did you have a nice sleep, Mr. Weber?"

At that point, I was beginning to realize I was in some deep shit. After slugging me in the face and knocking me down, he ordered me to face the 120 soldiers standing in front of me and apologize to them for oversleeping. Following that, he told all the trainees to lay on their backs on the rocky gravel with their arms and legs up.

This was called the *dying-cockroach position*. It was an almost-impossible position to hold for very long, especially if it was a hot, sunny day. It was about ninety degrees that day. After a few minutes, I was instructed to laugh at them. It was either that, or I would be kicked out of the army. Following orders is the law in the military. As I walked around the 120 soldiers, I laughed as hard as I could. After about fifteen minutes, the soldiers were sweating and cursing. The sergeant looked at me and shouted one word as he walked away.

"Dismissed!"

Some of the soldiers started running toward me. As I was really fast, most of them couldn't catch me. However, a few of them did. I was taken into the barracks and given a *GI shower*. If you don't know what those are, don't ask. They are really bad. First, they rubbed lye soap on me, which can sting and cause chemical burns. It is mostly used for cleaning purposes. After that, they put me in a really hot shower and scrubbed me with wire brushes. I really hurt and I bled some, but I didn't blame them. Needless to say, I never overslept after that.

About a month into my early training, I was walking over to one of the offices, and I noticed a woman walking toward me. She was in a really nice-looking uniform and was pretty cute too. I smiled at her and walked on by. *Oops.*

"Get over here!"

Once again, I was beginning to feel like I was in trouble once more.

"What do you say to me?"

I noticed bars on her soldiers, indicating she must have been an officer. But I had never seen a woman soldier, let alone a woman officer. I quickly stood at attention and saluted.

"Yes, sir. I am sorry, sir." *Jesus, Ron. Why can't you just shut your mouth?*

"Sir? Sir? Do I look like a man to you?

"I am really sorry. I have never seen a woman officer and don't know what to say?"

"Ma'am, goddamn you! Ma'am!"

"Yes, ma'am."

At that point, I was ordered to walk over and stand in front of a phone pole. I was to salute the pole and shout, "Good morning, Ma'am!" for the following four hours. I was covered in sweat and ready to die. Finally, she walked out of her office and dismissed me. Later that day, my sergeant heard about it and called me into his office.

"So, Ronnie, did you learn anything from all that?"

"Yes, sir, I did."

"Good. I want you to... What do I see? Is that chewing gum I see in your mouth? You know gum is illegal in Basic Training, do you not?"

"No, sir, I did not know that."

"Well, Weber, now you do."

I knew something bad was coming. I couldn't wait. I was ordered to dig a grave three feet by eight feet, and six feet deep. This was the standard-size grave for a human being. It took me about six hours, and I was exhausted. Then I was told to throw the gum the sergeant had taken from me earlier into the grave and bury it. That only took about an hour, and I was so tired I thought I was going to die. No more gum for Ronnie. The only thing good out of all this is that I now understood I could not beat the United States Army. I had to behave or get out. I always continued to be a little Irish prankster, but I made sure I obeyed commands and stay out of big trouble. However, when I went overseas, everything changed. When you are stationed in places like Vietnam, Korea, or the Middle East, a lot of the officers quit being so hard on the soldiers. Being where they were was punishment enough.

11. Naked in Korea

The Quonset huts we lived in at our base in Korea were these small tin cans with no windows. They were dark and depressing. There were just two rows of cots with two diesel heaters in the middle, one near each end. The lights were dim, and the diesel stank so bad that it was hard to sleep. During the long winters the temperatures dropped to a minus twenty or less. Up north near the DMZ, the winds would howl as they blew across the plains and hills, making the wind-chill factor even lower. Those tin huts had no insulation whatsoever. They were just constructed with thin sheet metal. They looked like soup cans cut in half and laid on their side with a door on each end.

When I walked in there for the first time, I wanted to cry. I was just this eighteen-year-old immature kid and missed my big bedroom at home. I soon discovered that no one there wanted to be thousands of miles away from their family and friends. As I entered the hut, about a dozen guys in military khakis, sitting on their cots, stared at me. I was carrying a huge duffel bag with all my belongings in it. All I had was army clothing. That was all we had. Without a word I just stood there. One big guy pointed at an empty cot, where I was to spend the next year and a half. At the end of my cot was a footlocker, where I put my belongings. Then I just sat on the bed, wishing all this was a bad dream. Slowly, some of the guys came over and introduced themselves. Others paid no attention to me. The first guy who came over was a real friendly fellow from Maryland named Tim. He had a warm smile and was the kind of person who would look after new recruits. We became fast friends, and over fifty years later we are still friends. He too is suffering from the effects of exposure to Agent Orange. I worry about him all the time.

Holidays were the worst. At Christmastime Tim would play this song on a little cassette recorder. The title was, "Daddy's Home." It made every damn one of us hardened soldiers shed at least one tear. Every night we would go to a bar on the base or into the village outside the gates of Camp Casey, where we would drown our sorrows in beer. What helped me a lot was my Irish humor. I was always making people laugh. I had learned as a child that laughter was one of the greatest gifts ever given to us. It could be the best medicine for depression.

While we were there to keep the North Korean soldiers out of South Korea, we also had jobs. My first one was as a tower guard, which was one of the worst jobs there. You just stood there twenty feet up in the air in a little box, damn near freezing to death and waiting for the North Korean soldiers to come. Later I got to come out of the cold and work in an office. My last job was working in the base motor pool, taking care of the vehicles. Soon after I got there, I was introduced to a small Korean man, whom I was told was our house-boy. I believe his name was Kim. His job was to clean the inside of our Quonset hut, make our beds, and wash our dirty clothes. Every payday we would give him some money.

After a few months I noticed that some of my clothes were miss-ing. When I asked Tim about it, he warned me that because it was so cold in that part of Korea, some of the houseboys would take socks, underpants, T-shirts, and occasionally, a uniform. They could sell it in the village or keep it for themselves. I spoke to Kim about it, and he got really mad. He said he was not a "slicky boy" and resented me questioning his honesty. Slicky boys were Korean boys or adult males that stole. I first was introduced to them when I was brought to Camp Casey. They were running alongside our vehicles and grab-bing anything that wasn't tied down. I let my sergeant know about the missing clothing, but he just blew me off.

A month later I had more clothes missing. I complained to our sergeant again, and he did nothing about it as usual. The following morning the issue was dealt with immediately. In front of our head-quarters building was a large open lot. Every morning hundreds of American soldiers would stand in formation. We would be lined up like chess pieces on a board, standing tall and looking good with our uniforms in perfect condition. The sergeants, lieutenants, captains, majors, colonels, and every other high-ranking officer stood in front of us, looking for a missing button, a wrinkly uniform, shoes that weren't polished, or anything else that was not perfect. Then, name by name, we were called out, and we answered, "Here, sir!"

"Weber!"

Silence.

"Weber!"

Silence.

"Weber! Where in the hell is Weber?"

"Here, sir!"

At that point, the sergeant heard me, but I was not in forma-tion. He was looking for me and still calling my name. It was minus twenty degrees outside. Everyone wanted to go inside to their jobs, but they could not go until every soldier was accounted for. Where the hell was Ron Weber?

"Here, sir."

At that very moment, over two hundred soldiers broke out into hysterical laughter. Behind the sergeant, a butt-naked man walked out from one of the buildings. He didn't even have a single sock on his bare feet. There I was, standing at attention as though nothing was wrong. The officers tried to maintain a professional appearance. The only one that could not was my sergeant. He ran over and started screaming at the top of his lungs for me to get back inside my hut and put some clothes on. I informed him that the slicky boy had taken them—all of them.

"I don't have any clothes, sir."

While I did have some clothes left, I was just making a point. I wanted the sergeant to deal with this stealing by our houseboy. After my stunt, he did. An hour later I was in a fresh, new uniform with extras in my locker. Our houseboy was fired. I was confined to my hut for ten days for public nudity. I was also the most popular guy on the base after that.

12. Boots on the Ground

In the military, we used the expression *boots on the ground*: marching here, marching there, and everywhere else. Our boots were the most important part of our uniform. In tough situations, we could do without a hat or a shirt, but never could we be without our beloved boots. Fifty-plus years later, I still have my boots on the ground. But they are not on some military base or overseas. They are also not those ugly black leather military boots. They are colorful and comfortable boots that can carry me up and down any steep trails or glide me for days out in the wilderness without blisters. Today and throughout a lot of yesterdays, my boots have been on hiking trails everywhere I go. I also have a sticker on my car's windshield that says, *My Other Car is a Pair of Hiking Boots.*

Besides climbing mountains, there were a lot of other physical things to do. I think my favorite hobby of all times has been hiking. In the woods, I talk to the trees and thank them for the oxygen they give out. I also find God in the forests and have had many long talks with him out there. I feel his spirit throughout the beautiful forests. I started walking on a trail behind our house at around the age of four or five. The trail was very steep and covered two small creeks, known as the first creek and the second creek. At the end of this trail was a street that bordered a small eighteen-hole golf course. Across the parking lot was the Oregon Zoo. Nearby was the beginning of the Wildwood hiking trail, which was over thirty miles long. All this was set in Portland, Oregon's Forest Park. This park was the largest urban park in the United States and consisted of seven thousand acres of stunningly beautiful woods. The trailhead of the Wildwood was only fifteen minutes from our house. It started next to a popular water tower in the Hoyt Arboretum Park, where a Vietnam Veterans Memorial resides today.

Often, we would hike up there or ride our bicycles. Then we just ran all over the woods until we were hungry and went home. Decades later, I still walk those trails. I have hiked on the Wildwood Trail around three thousand times, starting in the mid1950s. I have traveled close to ten thousand miles on this trail, usually in about five-to-ten-mile segments. This park is in my blood and a part of my soul. If I live to a hundred, I will be up there with a walker.

I have taken thousands of hikes in the beautiful Northwest Oregon and Southwest Washington over my lifetime. I have climbed mountains, ran marathons, backpacked, rode bicycles, and hiked all over the West Coast and throughout the world. My wife and me have traveled a lot, and wherever we go, I put my boots on the ground and enjoy the beautiful scenery. Numerous times in Mexico and the Caribbean, my wife stood nervously on the deck of many cruise ships. She stares up into the hills as the last of the passengers enter the boat. It is time for the ship to move to another beautiful port. But where in the hell is her husband? Off in the distance, I hear the large horn going off loudly. My boots suddenly start running, dragging me as fast as they can run. Down the hill and past the souvenir shops

I go. Once or twice, it looked like I was going to miss the boat and would have to take a private airplane to the next port. But I always seemed to make it just in time. Up on deck, Lydia would give me a bit of a frown and then ask me if I had a good hike. The answer was always *yes*. I always made an adventure of it. I would leave the ship, walk through the souvenir shops, and look up to the surrounding hills. For decades, I would just look for the highest hilltop and head in that directions. Locals often commented that the people on the cruise ships are supposed to stay near the shops and avoid the local towns. I believe the locals didn't want the rich tourists invading their privacy. Often, they lived in shacks and might have been embarrassed when tourists saw how they lived. I always told anyone who asked me what I was doing there. I would just point up to the hills and tell them I was a hiker. They seemed satisfied, and I continued on. Only once did someone come after me. A man was sitting outside, enjoying the day and a cold beer. He ran over to me and told me to get out of there. I kept walking, and soon, two more men ran over to me. I told them I was going to hike up in the hills, but they protested and said I was going nowhere except back to the ship. I looked at the three men and told them if they could catch me, I would leave. As I was a really fast runner, I just left them in the dust.

On my way up to the top of the small mountain, I suddenly heard a terrible hissing sound. When I turned to see what I thought would be a snake, I had a stick in my hand and prepared for a fight. To my surprise, it was not a snake. Instead, it was this large hideous-looking lizard of sorts. It was a few feet long and was the largest lizard-looking animal I had ever seen. Although it was low to the ground, it was about the size of a pit bull. I thought about running, but I was not sure how fast it could. I just stood still for a minute and started walking away slowly. I had seen locals carrying these animals around the souvenir shops and on beaches, charging money while tourists would hold them and have their pictures taken. They were beautiful and colorful. However, the one staring me down was big and orange. When I was about twenty feet away, it started to back into its hole in some rocks. That scared the crap out of me, but I kept on hiking. The views up there were stunning. On the way back to the cruise ship, I saw those three guys, still sipping beer at the outdoor bar. I walked over there without them noticing me and waved to the waitress. I gave her a twenty-dollar bill and told her it was for the guys who were chasing me. I waited at a distance until she went to their table. They listened to her and then looked over at me. Their frowns turn into big smiles and waved at me. I walked back through the shops and saw a man with one of those critters. I talked to him about it, and he told me that the vendors normally use females because they were less aggressive and were more colorful. He told me that they were iguanas, and that I had encountered a male out in the hills. He might have had a family nearby and was just protecting them. Being way out there in the hills, he might not have ever seen a human before. He was probably as scared as I was. Relieved that I wasn't attacked by him, I headed back to the boat and had another story to tell.

One of my all-time favorite hiking/backpacking trips was in the Trinity Alps of Northern California. Lydia met her sister and extended family at Trinity Lake every year for over thirty years. They always went in mid-to-late July. I got bored with just sitting in a boat on Trinity Lake (also known as Clare Engle Lake). So I would go hiking. I had made fifteen trips up there over a period of about thirty years and usually went to a spot named Stuart Fork Trail. It is a good twenty or more miles from the little town of Trinity on the way to Weaverville. The trail leads to a huge flat area, a half a mile long and a quarter of a mile wide. It was a stunning and huge plateau. It took me about eight hours to hike all the way up to this mountain-top meadow with over forty pounds on my back. At the top, I would set up a base camp. After that long haul, I would eat something and go to sleep. In the following days, I would hike up to an incredible lake, about four hours from base camp. Then about another four-plus hours up to a second lake. Years ago, I found a naked young woman swimming in the lake. No kidding. She invited me to come in, so I did. No funny business went on, but the water felt good as the temperature in July was usually about a hundred degrees in the afternoon.

After a couple of days or so at the meadow and the lakes, I would go east for about three days. I would walk all the way up to the top of different peaks in the Trinity Alps. I would spend at least two nights on rock as that was all there was up there. The last time I went up there was about ten years ago, when my health had improved. This time, I carried nothing. I decided to try something different. Normally, I would leave the Stuart Fork Camp, walk for about ten minutes, then turn around and go back to the car. I would start taking things out as the weight in the backpack was too much. So, this last time, I took a very small fanny pack with pepperoni sticks and other dried meats. Other than that, I only had a collapsing water cup, with those water purification pills. I would just drink the stream water, which was plentiful. I had about three pounds in my fanny pack, and that was it. Without any weight on my back, I practically ran up the trail and got to the meadow in about six or seven hours. At around 5:00 a.m. the following day, I walked up to the lakes (no naked lady this time). Then I slept another night at the meadow and headed up to the rocks. Beyond the meadow, going east, all the foliage was gone. Just hard rocks. Sleeping on the rocks with no pad or sleeping bag was challenging, especially on loose shale. This time, I decided to do something different. Instead of going back the way I came, I just took off into nowhere. After about a week, I was really getting low on dried meat, and I was exhausted from all the hiking. I found a creek and followed it down. From around 4:00 a.m. to midday, I just kept going. I finally found a logging road and followed it down to a paved road. I was so tired I started hitchhiking as I was about ten miles from my car.

Just minutes from when I started walking on this road, I saw a California Highway Patrol officer. He pulled over and wanted to know what I was doing walking way out in the boonies. I told him my tale, and he let me ride in the back. He was really friendly and was asking all these questions, like my name and where I was from. Little did I know that he was putting my information in his computer to see if I had any outstanding warrants, a practice that police personnel do on a regular basis. Suddenly, Officer Friendly slammed on his brakes, got out of the car, opened the back door, and started yelling at me. I was completely surprised and was almost speechless. He had found me on his computer data, and it said that I had a license to carry a handgun. Purchasing a gun was something I had done a long time before. I only had the gun for a year and turned it in to a local police department when we started having small grand-children around the house. However, the information was still in Oregon's computer base. He told me that I could have shot him in the back of the head if I been carrying a gun. The officer then told me that I was supposed to let him know that I had a license to carry a weapon, and whether or not I had one in my possession at this time. Although it made perfect sense to me, I had not owned a gun for about a decade, and it was something that was not on my mind. After a thorough balling out, he told me that I could walk the rest of the way to my car and think about what I had done (or had not done in this case). He also told me that hitchhiking was illegal there, and if he saw me doing it, he would arrest me. I limped the last five miles, grumbling all the way. When I got to my car, I collapsed and took a short nap. I wasn't mad at the cop as he was just doing his job. All in all, it was a good hiking and backpacking trip. In my seventies now, I don't take trips that long. They're just too much for me.

Another difficult backpacking trip was on Mount Jefferson in Oregon, just a few years ago. After a long trip up, I reached an area where there were three beautiful small lakes. I walked to all three and finally settled at one of them. I had been warned that it was fire season, and there was a fire not too far away, but it didn't seem close, and there were lots of people hiking up there. At the top, there were over a hundred people and tents everywhere. We could see a small fire, but it appeared to be far enough away and no danger to us.

About an hour later, a helicopter landed a short distance away. On a loudspeaker, we were told to leave. The fire was advancing toward us, and everyone quickly packed up. In about ten or fifteen minutes, the place was like a graveyard. The helicopter had left and so had all the people, except me. I was pissed as I hardly had any time to rest after the long haul up there. I also wanted to climb to the top of Mount Jefferson in a day or two, and I was already about a quarter of the way up. The thought of going all the way back to the parking lot and then going back up after the fire was contained really made me mad. Sitting right next to the largest of the three lakes, I pondered what I should do.

Then it hit me. The woods nearby were very small and measured only about 20 percent of the overall length of the lake. I decided to just stay there, and if the fire made it over to my camp, I had three options. The first was just to back off to the other lakes that had no trees around them. The second was to just stay near the lake and wait it out. If the fire got close, I would just get in the water with a wet rag over my face. The third option was to just run. As a former marathon runner, I could make it down that trail quickly. I decided to just wait. I climbed in my tent, and just about the time I was drifting off into sleep, I heard a horrible noise. I stuck my head out of the tent, only to see a helicopter headed right for me. Within seconds, the chopper was right on top of me. I got out of the tent and waited to get a thorough balling out from the pilot. Before I could surrender, I noticed a huge object attached to the helicopter headed right for me. It looked like one of those rescue buckets. It was the size of a car and coming right at me. I prepared to get hauled out by the bucket. It kept coming right at me, and just before I was going to get smashed to pieces, I jumped away and laid flat of the ground. The bucket went about thirty or forty feet away from me and fell into the water. I thought this chopper pilot didn't know how to fly that thing. Suddenly, I realized what was going on. The helicopter had no idea I was down there in the dark. He or she was dropping a water bucket to go fight the fire.

After the bucket filled up with water, the chopper flew off to dump it on the fire. About every fifteen minutes, the helicopter would get another bucket of water and continued on fighting the fire. I sat up and watched the show for about two hours. Then it all stopped. I went back in the tent and went to sleep. About 6:00 a.m., I was awakened by voices. Over the next few hours, I watched hundreds of people return and set up their camps. The fire was out, and things went back to normal. But I was just burned out about the whole event. I packed up and went home. I would come back the next year and try it again.

Despite a few tough times out in the wilderness, most experiences were somewhere between great and fantastic. I have spent a whole lifetime enjoying fresh air and good exercise. Beyond a shadow of a doubt, all of this made my life stronger and more enjoyable. I wouldn't trade a minute of it for anything else. I have seen scenery that can only be found by going there. Pictures are nice, but seeing it firsthand is a whole lot better. If you get out there and see an old guy with walking poles, it might just be me. In fact, I hope I do see you there. I like to meet you.

13. GUKA

In the winter of 2002, I was asked to be *Guka* for an unborn child. An African American best friend of mine had married a Kenyan lady and she was pregnant. Andre and Wambui soon had a little boy named Jaheem. Wambui was from the Kikuyu Tribe in Kenya and *Guka* meant *Grandfather*. I was both thrilled and honored. Later, Andre and Wambui brought me another boy, Jaleel. Over the years, I became *Grampa* to over twenty kids in a large Kenyan and African-American community of Jaheem and Jaleel's cousins. Most all of them and their parents live close by. Today they range from the first grade to college age. No doubt I am the busiest and happiest Grampa in the world. But that is for another book. I'm working on it.

CONCLUSION

What is interesting is the fact that I got so sick for so long, and yet now I enjoy climbing, hiking, bicycling, and playing with the kids. It is like I wasn't really sick all those years, and maybe it was just a bad dream. However, I was truly sick for a long time, and it took a lot of strength to get through all my struggles. But I didn't do it alone. I had a lot of help. The doctors, surgeons, nurses, physical therapists, and medications all played a part. So did a loving wife and a patient god. Something else, too, is that we get a lot of good things from our parents that we don't even notice until we are older. For example, my mother taught me how to write and how to laugh, especially at difficult times. She really knew how to face adversity with strength and courage. I have always loved her for that, and I was able to tell her before she died. Suddenly, this morning I also realized that the character and stubbornness that helped me with my VA case and getting through all the health problems not only came from my mom, but they also came from my dad. In the boxing ring of life, the guy that I hated for his drunkenness and violent temper turned out to be one of my best advocates. He was my coach through despair and frustration. Thanks, Dad. There is something I never told you while you were alive—I love you.

The irony of the whole thing is that after being such a naughty little boy, Freckles turned out okay. My wife, Lydia, and I have been married nearly half a century. Without her and a loving god, I would probably have ended up in the gutter. We have two great sons, a wonderful daughter-in-law, and are blessed with awesome grandchildren. We both had good careers and have a host of wonderful friends. We have been financially fortunate and have a comfortable life. It gets no better than that.

ABOUT THE AUTHOR

Ron Weber is a retired businessman, tradesman, and college teacher. He lives with his wife, Lydia, of nearly fifty years, just outside Portland, Oregon. Ron climbed mountains for fifty years. Today he enjoys hiking, bicycling, and writing.

For decades he accumulated stories about his life as little Ronnie Weber, also known as Freckles. Before the personal computers were born, Ron wrote stories by hand. In the 1970s he started using an IBM electric typewriter until computers helped him on his journey. He also wrote part-time for newspapers for over twenty years. Ron's love for writing sprang from his mother, who was both a college professor and a published writer.